Success Guide for the

UNSTOPPABLE
ENTREPRENEUR

A straightforward guide to help new business owners and entrepreneurs excel in their business.

Published By:
Unstoppable Publishing Company
430 E. 162nd St #330
South Holland, IL. 60473

Front Cover Design:
Julie Trotter Clark
Brand & Design Expert
President /CEO of
JT Clark Design
www.JTClark.com
Julie@JTClark.com

Back Cover Design:
Sandra Ballenger
sandraba@msn.com

Editor:
Erika Gilchrist

ISBN: 978-0-9838223-4-9

Other books available for purchase in the
Unstoppable Publishing's Library:

10 Ways to Prevent Failure (Audio Book)
*A straightforward guide to help you stay focused
on attaining your goals.*

Starting Today
*365 quotations to stimulate, inspire, and enhance
your personal growth.*

The Secrets to Being an Unstoppable Woman
*How to roll up your sleeves, make no excuses,
and get what you want!*

The Unstoppable Woman's Guide to
Emotional Well-Being
*A book for women written by 23 unstoppable female
authors, coaches, and professionals to help you establish and
maintain emotional wellness.*

How to Write & Publish Your Book NOW!!

If You Leave, I Will Kill You!
*Getting Off the **Beaten** Path of Domestic Violence*

www.TheUnstoppableWoman.net/library
866-443-6769
info@theunstoppablewoman.net

FOREWORD

An entrepreneur is a rare breed. Equal parts courageous, ambitious, naïve, and optimistic, few possess the traits and talent needed to succeed in the ultra-competitive world known as business.

I strongly believe that entrepreneurs are born, not made. An entrepreneurial fire is unique and cannot be taught. It is either ingrained within your DNA or it's not.

While a good education can help with the basics, equating business success to having a diploma is as misguided as suggesting that anyone with a driver's license has the potential to win the Indianapolis 500. The pedigree is seldom a predictor of achievement.

In an ideal world, everyone who creates their own endeavor would thrive. The harsh reality, however, is that most businesses fail and even those with the best intentions can find themselves broke, frustrated, and concerned about where their next meal is coming from.

Fortunately, Erika Gilchrist has assembled many of the world's foremost business experts who selflessly share their knowledge so you can avoid the mistakes they had to endure and offer their proven best practices which have helped them to prosper.

Business, like life, isn't easy. But, if you follow the advice found within these pages, you have significantly increased your odds of winning.

Ultimately, it is incredibly easy to be a critic, and unbelievably difficult to be a creator. I challenge you to become a creator and leverage the tips, tools, strategies, and shortcuts found within these invaluable pages to create an endeavor that massively impacts our world.

So, if you're one of the few, the proud, the brave, and the bold who consciously chooses to move from worker bee to boss, Erika Gilchrist's *The Success Guide for the Unstoppable Entrepreneur*, is your go-to resource for expeditiously attaining your desired results.

The world is waiting for you.

Live bold and *prophet!*

Steve Olsher
Entrepreneur, Keynote Speaker, and Author of *Internet Prophets: The World's Leading Experts Reveal How to Profit Online* and *Journey To You: A Step-by-Step Guide to Becoming Who You Were Born to Be*

The Editor

Assaulted as a little girl, sleeping in a van with her ex-husband, and living in a women's shelter, Erika Gilchrist has earn the title of *"The Unstoppable Woman."* She is regarded as one of the most energizing, engaging, and captivating speakers in the industry.
She is the Producer & Host of WTF – **W**omen **T**hriving **F**earlessly!, an online television talk show which can be seen at WomenThrivingFearlessly.com. Erika spends her life creating a global revolution of unstoppable women through her events for women focusing on personal and professional development. [TheUnstoppableWoman.net] As a published author of 9 books, she empowers entrepreneurs and professionals by teaching them how to position themselves as experts through her workshops & mastermind groups, "How to Write & Publish Your Own Book." [CompleteThatBook.com] She's been featured as one of the *"15 Most Powerful Women on the South Side of Chicago,"* CLTV, and Rolling Out Magazine.

Erika travels across the globe delivering keynote speeches, workshops, and panel discussions that inspire her audiences to move into action. "It's important to me to provide value to the lives of others, even if they never spend a dime with me."

www.TheUnstoppableWoman.net - info@theunstoppablewoman.net

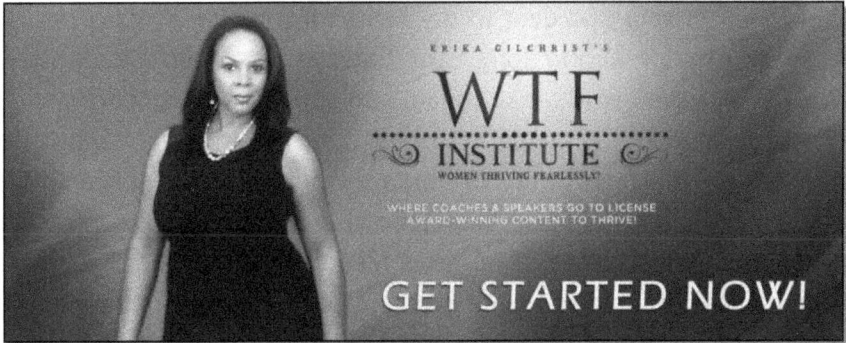

<u>INTRODUCTION</u>

This book is near and dear to my heart for a number of reasons. I have known for a very long time that having a job that dictates what time I start work, take lunch, and end work wasn't for me. I am not someone who enjoys predictability, especially when it comes to how I contribute my gifts to the world. I am drawn to spontaneity, and adventure. So it's no wonder that I absolutely love being an entrepreneur and business owner. In shaky economic and global times, the path became even clearer. Working for another is now more unstable than working for yourself.

I know there are other people in the world who feel the same way I do. I know there are others who can't fathom "regular business hours." I wanted to reach them and encourage them to stay the path, and remain focused. I wanted to create something that would offer real resources to assist business owners and entrepreneurs in being self sufficient. But I knew I couldn't do it alone; this book, is that answer.

Assembled here you will find a stellar group of authors, business owners, and entrepreneurs who have learned how not to just tread waters, but to swim swiftly. They have experienced the risks and rewards of entrepreneurship and they're eager, just as I am, to share their insights with the world.

Readers, I am proud to present this book as a constant resource in your library to support your venture in being an accomplished, profitable, and fulfilled entrepreneur. Here's to your success!

Erika Gilchrist
Award-Winning Speaker & Acclaimed Author

TABLE OF CONTENTS

Dr. Wilkins has provided unparalleled professional training, personal and business consulting for over 20 years. He is a best-selling author, and founder of three of the most comprehensive not for profit training associations in the country (**SPAA** – Speakers Publishers & Authors Association, **NAASA**-National African American Speakers Association, & **YSA** – Young Speakers Association). He is also the President of *Wilkins & Associates,* and Senior Pastor of *Created By Christ Ministries* and *CBC Productions* a professional theater company.

Dr. Wilkins has earned two Ph.D.'s (One in Accounting and the other in Theology), and lives the life he speaks about. Consequently, in his book, *"No Secrets to Success,"* he offers realistic principles based upon tri-fold empowerment principles (Family, Economic & Spiritual Empowerment) he created after over twenty years of research. Dr. Wilkins has also developed a national *"Speak for Yourself!"* program, which includes his book (and training program) on bullying, as well as a national (self-help) radio and television program. He has lived his life according to his philosophy that, *"Those Who Say It Can't be Done, Should Never Interrupt Those (of us) Who Are Doing It*!*"* He sincerely believes that God gives large revelations to small people, so he encourages everyone he meets to believe in themselves over what others are believing about the economy. Consequently, he puts his money where his mouth is by offering opportunities for novice and professional speakers, as well as first-time or experienced authors to become paid professional speakers (trainers & consultants) or publish books for those who have been hindered by publishing costs. Dr. Wilkins leaves this challenge *"Do Something Today, That Others Won't, To Have Something Tomorrow That Others Don't!"*

Chapter 1

Transitioning from Employee to Entrepreneur

Dr. Michael V. Wilkins, Sr.

YOU'RE FIRED!

There are only two words that separate you from being an employee and becoming an entrepreneur; "You're Fired!" Different people transition from employee to entrepreneur for different reasons. Unfortunately, too many people are still hanging onto jobs that they no longer have any passion for. Furthermore, as a result of the current economic downturn many have been forced to transition regardless as to whether they were ready or not.

I am currently the author of over fourteen books, (from business development to developing personal relationships). I am currently the owner of two international and four successful national business enterprises. I have personally assisted literally hundreds of people succeed in starting and then sustaining a successful business. The one thing that most successful entrepreneurs have in common is an unstoppable passion to do what others say can't be done.

Regardless as to whether your transition was of your own initiative (or if you are still punching a clock with dreams of submitting the resignation letter you have been carrying around for the past six months), or whether the economy assisted you against your will, this is the best time to look forward to new opportunities as an entrepreneur.

When transitioning to entrepreneurship regardless as to why, there are at least three things that you must do in order to significantly increase the chances of you achieving sustainable success in your chosen field.

FIRST:

If you are currently still employed, before you make that leap of faith answer the following questions:

- ➢ Will you be able to maintain your current standard of living for the next six months or more?

- ➢ Is the current income from your employment necessary to meet your current obligations?

- ➢ Have you developed a detailed 'written' business plan pertaining to your desired business, product or service?

> ➤ Do you have a specific marketing plan for your business, product or service?

> ➤ Do you have the necessary discipline and passion to work for the best or worst boss there is - yourself?
> ➤ Finally, "Are you crazy?"

Despite what you think, these are all legitimate questions, especially the last one. Think about it, you almost have to be at least a little crazy, to leave a secure place of employment, for the possibility of running your own business. Like too many others, you can easily hide in your current employment situation by; watching the clock, dodging work, blaming others for all that's wrong at that job, developing ulcers from worrying, taking your frustrations out on family members and many of the other things you do as you continue to do just enough work to keep from being fired and are living just enough for the city.

On the other hand, if all you can think, dream, and scheme about is working for self, if your passion to become an entrepreneur is only surpassed by your passion for God (and hopefully family) then you are probably ready to make that proverbial leap.

Second:
If you were forced out (through premature termination, a layoff, downsizing, or what other terminology currently being used for those two words; "You're fired!") you still must answer the questions above plus the following;

> ➤ Do you qualify for any type of unemployment compensation (Even if you have been told "no" by your employer, I would check, unemployment claims go against

the employers account, if you don't claim unemployment, the employer may benefit)?

➢ Do you have a support system in place to help you through the rough times (financially and socially) in beginning your quest into entrepreneurship?

➢ Will you choose to do your business, product or service if you were not planning on getting paid to do it?

➢ Can you continue to work at a "9 to 5" job and start your business "on the side"?

➢ What do you have to lose?

Trying times (such as being let go from your place of employment) can actually be a blessing in disguise. I hate being the one to bring up the old cliché about making lemonade when life gives you lemons, but...it's true. This may be the perfect opportunity to accomplish that thing that you have been dreaming about for years.

Third:
If you have honestly answered the questions above and made an honest assessment of your ability to become an entrepreneur then the following is a few proven ideas to help you achieve the success you desire.

A. Decide the name of your business, product or service. This is not always an easy thing to do. A great deal of thought should go into deciding upon a name because this name must in some manner reflect your passion.

B. Decide whether you will become a "For-Profit" or "Not-for-Profit" business. Details of the definition of each can be found in the referenced resource in item "C" below.

C. Decide what type of entity you will become; A "Sole Proprietor" (You and the business are one and the same), A "S-Corporation", (75 employees or less), A "LLC" (Limited Liability Corporation), and/or a "C-Corporation" details of all of these can found in the book titled "The Incorporation Starter Kit" (**www.wilkins-associates.com**)

D. Retain a good and professional attorney and accountant; if you are knowledgeable in financial and accounting matters that is helpful, however, I always recommend allowing those who have expertise in the areas that you don't have expertise in, do those things that you won't (or can't) do.

E. Develop a good workable business plan (note that any good plan still needs to be updated every 6 months or so to remain useful), there are various types of software available to assist you with writing your own. You may also depending upon the type of entity you choose have to develop "by-laws" and "articles of incorporation". You may also acquire the services of professionals who write business plans for others. Finally, you may also find a template of a detailed business plan (including samples of by-laws and articles of incorporations) in "The Incorporation Starter Kit" referred to above in item "C."

F. Develop a marketing plan. This step is just as important as any of the steps above. You could have the best business, product or service in the country but if no one knows about it or you, you (and your business) are just blowing in the wind. While many spend a sufficient amount of time (and money) on the above steps, they are usually exhausted (and financially drained) by the time they get to this important step. So allow me to spend the remaining portion of my allotted space to share with you some crucial marketing tips even (especially) when you have little or no money.

CRUCIAL MARKETING TIPS FOR YOU, WHEN TRANISTIONING FROM EMPLOYEE TO ENTREPRENEUR, EVEN (ESPECIALLY) WHEN YOU HAVE LITTLE OR NO MONEY:

To start, you must properly define marketing. Marketing is anything and everything that you do to positively promote your business, product or service.

If your budget is tight and you insist on taking on entrepreneurship, I applaud you (All those who weren't serious or not sure, they never even made it this far). Here's how you do it;

1. **Identify and know your target market**. It's crucial that you know exactly who needs your product or service. Mass marketing doesn't work in today's business environment. Not only does it force you to water down your marketing message to please those you may not even want to reach, but it's much too expensive for anyone on a shoestring budget.

2. **Marketing is much like breathing**. It's the life of your small business and should be a regular part of your daily business activities. Research suggests that prospects need to encounter your small business between seven and twelve times before they are ready to purchase. So, put yourself in front of your target market over and over again. In today's internet and social media age, there are now more low-cost marketing options than ever before. You must tell everyone you know, everyone you meet and everyone in your social network circle, what you do and why they should do business with you. Develop a 30-second commercial (often referred to as the elevator pitch) that concisely says not what you do or sell but why you, your product or service can meet their needs. Not only is it possible, it is absolutely doable to substantially grow your small business on a small budget.

3. **Relationships.** As the founder of one of the fastest growing professional speaking, publishing and writing associations in the country (The Speakers Publishers & Authors Association, **www.thespaa.org**) I do not allow our members to use the "N" Word (Networking). The reason for this is the fact that it is essential for you to learn the importance of developing real "Relationships". Create real relationships with your prospects and customers. Answer their questions, solve their problems and help them if they're stuck. Your prospects want to know that there's a real person in front of your small business. What are you doing to get noticed? How are you different than your competition? The fastest way to small business failure is to blend in with the crowd. If your product and/or services aren't top quality, then you won't get repeat business. Your long-term success depends on satisfied customers who

spread the word about your business and purchase from you repeatedly. Position yourself as an expert and educate your prospects as to why your small business can offer them the remedy to their most pressing problems and/or concerns.

Things change quickly and you must be willing to adapt. When the next "great" marketing platform emerges, be willing to jump on board and embrace it with excitement. If you are a flexible entrepreneur, you'll learn to lead the way instead of always following the trends of others.

If your marketing is going to eventually take hold, then you need to make a strong commitment to see it through until it bears fruit. Don't give up in the early stages. The fruits of your marketing labors won't happen overnight. You need to plant your marketing seeds and tend to them regularly before your marketing garden blooms. Your clients and customers need to have a clear picture in their minds as to who you are and how your product or service can meet their needs.

As I close, I will be the first to admit that transitioning from employee to entrepreneur (and marketing) covers a multitude of other do's and don'ts, most of which can't be confined to the pages of this book. Therefore, I must also encourage you to get around like minded professionals, others who are pursuing their dreams of entrepreneurship. Join professional organizations like SPAA (The Speakers Publishers & Authors Association, **www.thespaa.org**), find a mentor that is doing what you want to do, and never ever allow anyone to discourage you from doing what you believe you are destined to do. Let me conclude by sharing with you a philosophy I developed; *"You must do something today that others won't, to have something tomorrow that others don't!'*

Susan Tolles is an *Expert in Midlife Reinventions* who inspires and equips women around the world to flourish inside and out. As a website creator, published author, speaker and life coach, Susan helps women celebrate and enrich their true inner and outer beauty as they age with grace and vitality.

Susan's website FlourishOver50.com, viewed by thousands of women globally each month, provides the resources and tools to make the second half of their lives their best, including articles and videos on style, health & fitness, food and wine, and life balance.

Susan's Powerful Me™ and individual coaching programs help women flourish from the inside out for a focused, purpose-driven future. Based on her own reinvention when she was a woman over 50 and an empty nester, Susan created her Powerful Me™ Program to help other women live in tune with their core passions and unique gifts, creating a future filled with joy and enthusiasm doing the things they love.

Susan is a published author, contributing to the collaborative books *Inspired Women Succeed* and *The Unstoppable Woman's Guide to Emotional Well-Being.* Both are available on her websites.

Susan lives in Austin, Texas, has been married for over 33 years and has three incredible children. She has worn many hats in her life and has personally experienced her own amazing midlife transformation, proving that it is never too late to discover your purpose and follow your dreams.

Contact Information:
www.FlourishOver50.com
www.MyPowerfulMe.com

susan@FlourishOver50.com

Chapter 2:

Establishing the Mission for Your Business

Susan Tolles

One of the most powerful things you can do to make your business successful is to have a mission statement. Whether you are a sole-proprietor or CEO of a Fortune 500 company, whether you are in the idea stage or a seasoned entrepreneur, you need a mission statement to provide yourself, your staff, and your customers with a clear picture of who you are, what you do, and why you do it. Without one, you are like a boat adrift without a compass or sail: you have no real direction.

WHY HAVE A MISSION STATEMENT?

When I began my journey as an entrepreneur, I really had no idea where to begin or what steps to take to get started (congratulations on using this book as *your* guide!). I had some great ideas, however, so I pitched them to a marketing coach and we took off on a path to create a successful business. While he was skillful at helping me define my customer profiles and create a beautiful logo, I never took time to understand the *why* and *how* of the plan. I only knew that I wanted to reach a large audience of women in my age group with an online magazine for women over 50, so I created a website, wrote content, and pushed myself relentlessly for a year.

At the end of that first year, I finally looked up, took a breath and realized that I wasn't even sure I was on the right path. Because there was no clear purpose for my business, I didn't know why I was doing what I was doing, and wasn't sure I should even keep going.

It was then that I took a break to go inward, to discover my "life purpose," my personal mission statement. Through that self-guided journey, I learned that living in alignment with my passions and values is what would sustain my energy and enthusiasm. Following where my soul directed me and letting my heart dream bigger dreams brought me an excitement and focus that I'd not experienced in months. I found I could match my passions and gifts with the needs of a group of people who were important to me. My life purpose would translate into the mission statement for my business, providing harmony between the personal and professional areas of my life.

Since that time of re-focusing and renewal, I have been organized, productive, and enthusiastic (almost) every day. . . I continue to grow and evolve into something better, always connected to my core purpose and confident that I am on the right path this time.

If I had not found my true purpose, I probably would have given up, frustrated and exhausted, throwing away all the hard work and effort that had been invested that first year. I might have found a job working for someone else, not being true to my own heart and soul. I would not be honoring God by using what He has so generously given me to make a difference in the lives of others.

Before creating the processes and products of your business, you have to know why you will be in business in the first place. Writing a powerful mission statement should be one of the first steps in your entrepreneurial journey, the "why" before the "how."

- A mission statement is the picture of your core purpose and values, the very reason for your business existence. Identifying what drives you, what "lights your fire," and what impact you want to make on others will keep you grounded. Trying to run a business that is inconsistent with these principles will be frustrating and unproductive, and your work will often seem meaningless.

- Keeping your mission statement in front of you and your employees is a great motivator and keeps everyone focused on what is truly important. If everyone understands and commits to your purpose, they, too, will be passionate about the overall business, from the smallest administrative details to the bigger things like sales and customer service.

- A mission statement provides the foundation for your business plan. By building your goals and strategies in alignment with your mission, you will stay focused on what is truly important. Setting goals that do not support your mission will cause you to waste precious time and energy and will not move you toward achieving success.

- A mission statement inspires you to persevere and stay focused. When times get tough, when you are weary or discouraged, or when seemingly insurmountable obstacles get in the way, reading your mission statement can "re-ignite the fire" as it reminds you of why you do what you do. Taking time to reflect on the mission you had when you began will give you new energy and commitment to keep going.

HOW TO BEGIN

How do you create your own mission statement? First, understand that this is not a one-hour exercise. It takes extended time and much thought to go through the process, but it will be well worth your effort. Here's how to get started.

- **Get away.** Spending time free from distractions will be essential to really digging deep. Plan a retreat, get out of your office, and block out sufficient time so you won't feel rushed.

- **Brainstorm freely.** Allow your creative self to be in control, putting your self-critic to the side for a while. Don't over-analyze your answers, and don't worry about the "how" for now. If you are really following your purpose or mission, the "how" will come easily later.

- **Seek input.** Even if you are a sole-proprietor, it is still valuable to have input from others. Ask a few trusted advisors or mentors to help along the way, from pointing out your strengths to refining your mission statement after it is crafted.

- **Find examples to guide you.** Reading mission statements of other successful businesses can provide you with some great ideas to begin with. Do an internet search for "mission statement examples," and sites such as MissionStatements.com can give you a jump start. A list of very powerful and inspiring mission statements is provided at the end of this chapter.

ANSWER THESE QUESTIONS

To craft a clearly articulated mission statement for your business, you first must answer a few questions. Get large sheets of paper and write your answers to the following question—again, without over-analyzing them. Allow your creativity to flow, and write from the heart. Include the things YOU want, not what others want for you.

1. Who are you?

- What are your passions? What "lights your fire?"
- What are your non-negotiable core values?

- What are your strengths and unique skills?
- What do you want for yourself and your customers?

2 **Who do others say you are?** Ask a close group of friends, family and business colleagues:
- When you hear my name, what are the first words that come to your mind?
- What are my strengths and weaknesses?
- What do you see me doing in the future?
- What do you NOT see me doing in the future?

You will see consistencies in some areas that will help you focus on the strengths and skills that you can build on. Make note of these trends and use them to build on.

3. What do you do?
- What product or service do you provide for your customer?
- What "pain points" or emotional needs do you solve?
- What physical need do you satisfy?
- What do *they want*? Remember, you are not your customer.

Answer these questions from your ideal customer's perspective, not just focusing on the product, but the entire experience they want to have. For example, Zappo's is the most popular internet shoe store. Zappo's Mission Statement is not just to sell shoes, it is to be *the online retail **service** leader*, knowing that exceptional customer service will drive sales more than just having a great selection of shoes. People want to be happy, to be cared for, and to receive special treatment and exceptional service. This is what the Zappo's experience is all about. Explore their website and you will see what makes them extremely popular with their customers.

Likewise, The American Cancer Society focuses on more than just curing cancer. They also include the physical and emotional needs of their "customers" in the organization's mission statement: *The American Cancer Society is the nationwide community-based voluntary health organization dedicated to eliminating cancer as a major health problem by preventing cancer, saving lives, and diminishing suffering from cancer, through research, education, advocacy, and service.*

4. **Who do you serve? What is your "niche?"**
   - What group of people are you most passionate about working with? Who do you enjoy helping?
   - Who will benefit most from your product or service? Whose lives will you impact?
   - What are the demographics of your customers, including age, sex, geographic region, income, and ethnicity?
   - What are each customer's personal (physical and emotional) characteristics? What is her name? What are her life circumstances?
   - Create several detailed descriptions of your target audience members that you can visualize so you can speak to them directly in your marketing efforts.

Remember, you cannot be all things to all people, so the more narrowly you define your target market, the easier it will be to serve them. Finding your niche will provide greater clarity and reduce stress since you don't have to understand so many market segments. You can always expand later when you are ready to grow your business.

5. **What impact do you want to make on the world?**
   - What are the needs of the marketplace that you will fulfill? What "greater good" do you want to serve?

- What is the cultural change you want to affect?

Another example is La Tienda, a fair-trade company in the Dominican Republic that sells jewelry. Their core purpose is not just to sell jewelry, but also to provide the women who work there with a means to support their families, saving them from prostitution and poverty. La Tienda's mission statement, as found on their website, says *La Tienda seeks to provide a fair trade opportunity to women carrying the burden of poverty in the Dominican Republic. The women make beautiful handmade items to sell in order to provide for their families.* The women make jewelry and accessories sold on the internet and in-home parties. The sales help combat the deep poverty in their communities.

BRING IT ALL TOGETHER

Now that you have spent time digging deeply into the who, why, and how of your business, it is time to write your own mission statement. Keep in mind:
- It should be clear, concise and free of jargon or industry-specific language that the general public would not understand.
- It should communicate your core purpose, the reason why you are doing what you do, with words that create a visual image that would motivate others to do business with you.
- It should create commitment and enthusiasm with your employees.
- It should provide the foundation for your goals and strategic plan.

Your mission statement will take time to write; it will evolve over weeks, even months. After your first draft is written, live with it for a while and see if it still feels comfortable and compelling when you come back to it later. Ask others if it is clear—do they understand what you do and why you do it? Would they want to do business with you? Seek feedback from employees—you need their support!—and from more experienced business colleagues. Be open to change as you grow, gain new perspectives, and learn more about your trade and your market.

When you have written a mission statement that conveys your purpose, values, and customers, then tell the world! Put it on your marketing materials, website, and business cards. Write a 60-second "introduction" including your mission statement and be ready when someone asks what you do. It should flow freely and inspire others to say, "Tell me more!"

My current mission statement took over a year to develop fully. The more I allowed myself to be creative and grow, the greater clarity I received. The more patient I was with the process, trusting my intuition and seeking the input of others, the more powerful my statement became. What first started as a broad vision that was difficult to conceptualize has now become the foundation for everything I do professionally.

I am an expert in midlife reinventions, using my God-given gifts to inspire and equip midlife women to flourish inside and out..

Defining your mission statement not only provides you with a clear and concise way of describing what you do, it takes you through a process that ensures you are honoring your purpose and are solidly committed to your business. You will come through these exercises knowing exactly where you are headed, who you will serve, and how you will honor your passions and values. With your mission statement, you will become an unstoppable entrepreneur, sailing through the open seas with your compass set for an exhilarating journey toward a successful future.

EXAMPLES OF MISSION STATEMENTS

Southwest Airlines

The mission of Southwest Airlines is dedication to the highest quality of Customer Service delivered with a sense of warmth, friendliness, individual pride, and Company Spirit.

Starbucks Coffee

Our mission: to inspire and nurture the human spirit – one person, one cup and one neighborhood at a time.

Nike

To bring inspiration and innovation to every athlete in the world. If you have a body, you are an athlete.

Google

Google's mission is to organize the world's information and make it universally accessible and useful.

McDonald's

McDonald's mission is to be the world's best quick service restaurant experience. Being the best means providing outstanding quality, service, cleanliness, and value, so that we make every customer in every restaurant smile.

Proctor & Gamble

We will provide branded products and services of superior quality and value that improve the lives of the world's consumers. As a result, consumers will reward us with leadership sales, profit, and value creation, allowing our people, our shareholders, and the communities in which we live and work to prosper.

Habitat for Humanity

Seeking to put God's love into action, Habitat for Humanity brings people together to build homes, communities and hope.

The Humane Society of the United States

To create a humane and sustainable world for all animals, including people, through education, advocacy, and the promotion of respect and compassion.

United States Department of Justice

To enforce the law and defend the interests of the United States according to the law; to ensure public safety against threats foreign and domestic; to provide federal leadership in preventing and controlling crime; to seek just punishment for those guilty of unlawful behavior; and to ensure fair and impartial administration of justice for all Americans.

Tony Robbins, Motivational Speaker and Author

The purpose of my life is to humbly serve our Lord by being a loving, playful, powerful, and passionate example of the absolute joy that is available to us the moment that we rejoice in God's gifts and sincerely love and enjoy all his creations.

Each mission statement was taken from the website of the respective company or individual.

Deb Damone is a life coach in family development, certified from Cornell University. She is also an accomplished poet and published writer. Her brand is "Trial to Triumph." Deb published her first autobiographical book: The Ominous Betrayal: Memoir of a child of hope in 2010, followed by its sequel, An Awesome Journey in 2011. In 2012 she was privileged to compile, contribute and aide in the editing of an anthology entitled: Mental Wellness: Real stories from Survivors. After creating her own mental health (not for profit) agency, PIPER-People Improving Peer Empowering Recovery in 2007, she closed it in 2011 due to a lack of funding. However, one of the projects birthed from PIPER was her work with the Hidden thoughts press on the Mental Wellness book. In addition to the release of The Success Guide for the Unstoppable Entrepreneur, 2012 brought the release of her first novel Bella Rosa's Portrait, in addition to the launching of another anthology, How to Create a Rich, Successful, and Fulfilling Life: Dynamic Tools for Overcoming Obstacles and Creating Rapid Transformation.

Deb married 40 years in June of 2012 to her high school sweetheart Dennis, marvels how fast the years have passed. They have two adult children, both of whom are married to wonderful people.

In addition to her writing, Deb continues to work with the broken hearted, broken families, as well as those who are starting up new businesses, and venturing into new territories.

Jewel of the Soul Life Coaching
Hauppauge, New York 11788
631-747-4197
http://www.DamoneJewel.com
http://www.debjdamone.com

Chapter 3

Considerations for the New Entrepreneur

Deb J. Damone

The ability to create is one of the most fascinating and exuberating accomplishments one can realize. You are the author and finisher of work displayed with pride. Such is the case within the world of the entrepreneur. We are creating a work environment that will bring in revenue that we have created from the ground up. It is like the amazing progression of a painting masterpiece from that first inkling, to the first stroke of the brush on a blank canvas. Planning is essential to success and formulating that positive image. This what will bring the right people at the right time; it's the law of attraction!

Projecting a positive business image is more than getting a good business card, snazzy brochures, a website and a five-cent line. Our objective is to reach out with ideas, products or services to touch and ripple into the lives of others while earning a living. Always be mindful that the vehicle that we choose promotes our professional image as we share with the world a glimpse of who we are. And therefore, it is critical that we project a positive business image, as it often represents us long before we meet potential clients in person. Though consistent with the idea that the early bird may get the proverbial worm, sure and steady is bound to be fruitful in due season with a boatload of fish, not just worms!

In the infant stages of business, many often fail due to lack of direction, misuse of time or lack of business savvy. There is much that can derail the eager business owner. One deterrent to facing these issues is determining what the destination looks like and how to arrive there. Preparation and goal planning of the company's image are tools to the entrepreneur, as is a map and compass to a sea captain.

No business can sport a polished professional appearance without organizational charts or well-laid plans. Learning from mistakes and progressing from those stepping-stones known as setbacks can be a schoolmaster enhancing knowledge for the future. Those who do not know how to readjust and tweak their business often remain off course and finish shipwrecked. Had those who were far adrift from their goals and destination reinstated a new plan or course of action, they might have gained that much needed momentum for success.

It's rudimentary to take inventory of where you are on a regular basis. Reevaluating goals often helps to clarify new alternatives for old choices. Often the course gets blurred with the everyday essentials to run things smoothly; nonetheless, a reaffirming glance at your map (plan) will once again bring you closer to your destination.

When in the process of creating any new work, a great deal of forethought accompanies a product of quality. No less is true in the creation of that profitable business. You have stepped out from the shadows to take on a remarkable task. There may be others in the same field, but there is only one you! And you are the core of the work.

The following seven strategies can support you when choosing a direction for your business to achieve greater success; streamlining the process for less apprehension. Consider each of them as you contemplate the type of business you will run.

Mindset

Volumes could be written about mindset, but for the purpose of this chapter we will divide it into two categories: confidence and professional etiquette.

Confidence-

Entrepreneurs need a definite mindset. The perception that you carry of yourself will spill over into your business. Whether you are selling your work on-line or in person, exuding confidence is essential. Confidence comes from two words, which mean "with faith," and translates into certainty. It is realizing what your capabilities are and having that certainty that you and your products or services can fulfill the assignment or task at hand. Here is where balance will be essential to success. Arrogance or hubris is not confidence. When either is enacted in business, there is almost always a reverse effect on people. So be careful to balance your know-how with humility.

Bringing your confidence to life:
1. Know your self worth
2. Have an attitude of gratitude
3. Be positive and upbeat about your work and towards others
4. Speak your truth with humility
5. Trust in what you know, but also have a teachable spirit
6. Know failure is a mere setback not defeat; it is another step towards success

Professional Etiquette-

Professional etiquette is an intricate part of standards that govern socially acceptable behaviors in the workplace. You can be stunning, uncanny, and utilize unconventional methods in your concepts, however professional etiquette must be maintained and will be optimal on your journey to success. Times and trends may change, but some things remain the same. Professional etiquette seems to be lacking in the developments of new technology, but nonetheless it is still essential to the entrepreneur. Below you'll find fundamentals that intelligent successful entrepreneurs adhere to:

1. Wear appropriate attire & dress for success - Be clean and polished from head to! First impressions are lasting impressions.

2. Language (Verbal & Body) - Swearing and dirty jokes still don't fly, no matter how progressive the times are. Keep your body language in accordance with good communication skills. Stand and sit tall; slouching sends a message of shoddiness or a lack of confidence.

3. Time Theft- It's often said that if you are on time you're considered late. **Remember that tardiness is theft**. You are stealing something you can never repay to another person...Their TIME!

4. Own your mistakes - Regardless of the situation, honesty is still the best policy. Take responsibility for your decisions and actions. You earn more respect from others when you admit fault.

5. Develop your handshake - Research indicates that a good handshake can increase the chances of landing that new client, sale etc.

6. Put down the cell phone! - You have agreed to this time with the   person you are meeting with; give them that time without the cell on your ear. It is rude and shows a lack of business savvy.

7. Be reliable - If you promise something always deliver. If you can't get to the work, or can't make an appointment on time, then contact the other party immediately to communicate the situation.

8. Develop a proper telephone greeting – Voice tone and inflection can be captivating or can cause disillusionment. Although people can't see you, attitude shows through to the person on the other end of the call. If you are smiling there is a positive inflection in the voice; the same is true of a bad attitude. Keep it upbeat!

9. Don't chew gum on appointments, during meetings or on the phone. Suck on a mint to freshen your mouth. There is nothing more distracting than bad breath.

10. Make eye contact - Here in the United States it is considered rude not to make direct eye contact. When eye contact is made, it expresses a positive image with strength of character.

11. Multicultural Savvy- From my research there was no mention of such an important point on any websites or in any books. However, with the Internet the world has literally opened up, while growing smaller for the entrepreneur to reach out to other lands. It is imperative to have an understanding of the culture that you are dealing with. Do NOT leave this to chance. If you have a universal business, learn business and social customs of those that you are dealing with.

12. During meetings, lean in towards the orator as they speak and give your undivided attention to them. Distractions such as rolling pens, clicking your pen, scanning the web, looking around the room etc. sends a message of disinterest to the one speaking. Be mindful to intentionally be present!

Discipline

Discipline or the lack there of can be the deciding factor of whether your business not only gets off the ground, but also stays afloat. Since there are no time clocks to punch and you are the boss, you need to put a schedule together. There are a number of reasons for this. Without a schedule you have no target. Without a target, which is your goal, you have no idea if you attained it. It is important to run consistent business hours according to the work that you do. If you are working with clients in China, and you're in the U.S., you need to set your schedule accordingly so you are available during their workday. It is also equally important to stop at a reasonable hour if you are a family person. I have seen many marriages hit the rocks because the work became their mistress or lover. It is discipline that sits you down at your desk to work, but it is also discipline that knows when to quit!

How to stay disciplined:
1. Work by a clock and a calendar
2. Create your workspace and keep it in order
3. Don't allow distractions to take you away from planned itinerary
4. Make sure that you keep the focus on your plan and goals

Décor

Décor is the outward indication of who you are. It can be the place where you have your business, your website or how you project your business image when meeting in person. Meeting in person means you and your portfolio are courting the prospective person of interest. As was mentioned, professional etiquette speaks through you and your appearance. But if you have a home office it is wise to remember that:

1. It should be clean and tidy and reflect what you want people to see. Unsightly used tissues, bed pillows or an un-vacuumed rug can distract from the ambiance of the room.
2. It should have good lighting and healthy air circulation.
3. It should include your work essentials to operate smoothly.
4. There shouldn't be noise levels causing distractions, such as children and TV sets blaring.
5. There should always be a reasonable sitting area for the clients or colleagues as you conduct your business.
6. It should reflect an aura of business. So even if you are at your dining room table, make sure that there is no clutter on the table. And that the table is clear of all food.

7. Whenever possible, it is best for a home business to allocate an area that is used exclusively for your business with a separate entrance.

Your website is also part of the décor. It is the one place where thousands of people can come and find out about you, your brand and whom you are trying to influence. The general rule is to make it clear, uncluttered and direct, not general information. This may be your only chance to reach that potential client/customer. Give them a clear presentation of your product or service.

Genre and Branding

Entrepreneurs must know what their brand, genre or niche is. To be able to convey your message, you must first be clear and concise as to what it is that you do. Your brand is what your message is to the world. In my case my brand is trials to triumph. Regardless of the situation that I am writing about or sharing in a presentation, I am always bringing the audience from the trial to the point of triumph. My autobiographies hone in on this method of branding as I take the reader from the beginning of my young life to the end in victory and hope. When people are looking for you on the Internet, what is your brand? Clarity of what you offer brings the appropriate audience, translating into good time-management.

This brings us to niche or genre. This is your target audience; those who you will supply products or services to. As a life coach specializing in family development, my target audience or niche is the family. Who are you trying to reach? Sit down and write what you offer in a clear descript sentence. When people ask what you do, don't tell them what category your work is in.

For example if you are a massage therapist, tell them that you help people to move better. When they ask how, that is when you tell them that you have learned various methods of massage that work to create a healthier you. Personalize it. Make it about them!

Save the pitch for dessert

When the entrepreneur wants to offer services or products, there are various ways to go about it. For example, advertising on the Internet and through social networking is a direct and definitive way to get the word out. However, there is nothing like one to one networking. When meeting others for the first time it is monumental to save the pitch for dessert. What do I mean? There is an old saying, "People don't care what you have to say, until they know that you care." It reflects a simple truth; let people get to know you before you rush into your pitch about your amazing new product or service! No one likes to be sold to, but everyone wants to buy! People want to decide for themselves. If you appear pushy, you're liable to turn off a perspective client or buyer. Another adage is that, "People may not remember what you say, but they always remember how you made them feel." When a person is made to feel like they are the most important person in the room, they are more inclined to listen to what you have to say. However, this is not to say that anything but genuine honesty should be your value trademark. Always put on the other persons' shoes when you are talking to them and feel the connection. If it seems like it is going well and they ask for more information...share. If you feel like you have misread the signals and jumped in too soon...back off. Save the dessert, and enjoy the dinner.

Relationship Intelligence

Of all the must do's when starting a business, relationship intelligence is enormous and probably the tip that can't be driven home enough. It's essential to see *people* first and foremost; the sale will come later if you are perceived as genuine. Even if everything else is in place, relationships are the key to projecting your business to a wider customer base. The most important way to build any business is through word of mouth. Building a good reputation through quality service and customer care is the fundamental piece that brings it all together. In Proverbs 22:1 we read: "A good name is rather to be chosen than great riches." Even if all else is in place, the wise entrepreneur understands that building trust and good customer relations is essential. **Every entrepreneur is in the catering business!** Regardless of what you offer, whether it is products, services or both, catering to the customer, knowing their needs, and supplying them with the best services will send a message that will spread like wildfire by word of mouth. Customers, clients and colleagues who are spreading the word about your efforts and reliability are the least expensive, but most effective way to grow the positive business image.

In the book, *The Speed of Trust* by Stephen M.R. Covey, we find that all relationships including work related relationships are built on trust. Trustworthiness is what will grow the work and spread your positive image. When people feel like they can trust you, doors open. You are a person of integrity. A positive business image must have a good reputation preceding it. Your positive name and company's reputation are the backbone and foundation for growth. Every day you send out a message, and that message is your calling card, which conveys the attributes of who you are and what you offer through your business.

Surveillance and Renovations

After all has been set in place for the best empirical practices your business can offer, the business conscious entrepreneur learns to tweak and reevaluate the workings of the business plan. As technology moves ahead, you must move with it on the cutting edge for efficiency, advancement and increase. Analyze what is working and what isn't. If your business has moved to a plateau and now you want to take it to another level, find a business consultant who can bring it to the next phase.

Being satisfied with where you are is healthy and important. However, it is critical not to get complacent. It is the cutting edge entrepreneur who will be in the forefront in any chosen field. Make the necessary changes to reinforce image and growth. Even if you have labored for hours on something…if it isn't working…scrap it! You can always come back and revisit it in the future with a fresh perspective.

If you see that the climate for your old way of doing no longer serves you well, then you may find yourself left in the dust! The savvy entrepreneur keeps it professional, stays current, does their homework, and keeps it new and alive all while maintaining who they genuinely are.

If something isn't working it doesn't mean that you are a failure. Use obstacles and problems that arise as lessons. Thomas Edison said that he found over seven hundred ways not to make a light bulb before he made it work. How many people would have given up by the tenth time, let alone over seven hundred times? It is in what I call the surveillance (monitoring) of our work where we find the renovations for our plan and our goals. The surveillance allows us to see what must be tweaked and revised for optimal performance and professional projection.

In conclusion, it is significant to note that nothing worth having comes easy. This is your business, your baby, and you will pour yourself into it, at times stretching yourself beyond your wildest imagination. But at the end of the day when all is said and done, following the guidelines provided announces who you are without wavering, reflecting the profitable business that we all desire.

Jan Schochet is founder and CEO of Work Vibrant, LLC, where she helps small business owners be heard, be hired, get more clients and skyrocket their business to success. **www.workvibrant.com** You can download "7 Easy Strategies to Be Heard + Be Hired and Get More Clients" here: **www.workvibrant.com/strategies**

<u>Chapter 4</u>

Narrowing Your Area of Expertise

Jan Schochet

One of the best things about having your own business is that you get to be the architect of it. You get to decide what your business will be, how you'll make it work, and how much *you'll* work. You're the captain of your own ship.

To make sure that ship is sailing along on smooth waters, I'd like to tell you something to help you along the sometimes shaky waters that are out there.

A way for you to jumpstart your path to success is to narrow the area of expertise you offer your clients and customers and your prospective clients and customers.

That's what this chapter is all about and here's what you'll learn:
* ❖ Why you should narrow your expertise.
* ❖ Some examples of narrowed expertise.
* ❖ How to figure out ways to narrow your expertise.
* ❖ Getting the word out about your narrowed area of expertise, sometimes called "a niche," (pronounced "neesh").

Why Narrow? Why a Niche?
There are four main reasons to narrow your area of expertise, or "niche down."

First, you can't be all things to all people. There's just no way you can market to all the people out there you think you could help—you're not Coke® or General Mills®. Your advertising budget isn't unlimited, as theirs is. You need to specialize so you can reach clients much easier and more cost effectively.

As unlikely as it sounds, it's easier to reach a small, targeted group of people than it is to reach everyone. When you try to reach everyone, you really reach no one.

As strange as it sounds, when people learn about what you do in your niche, people you're not even marketing to will find out about you and raise their hands to be in your "tribe" of followers. They'll want to learn about what you do and how you help people.

Here's a surprising example of that: One of my clients is a relationship coach. She helps single women find the man of their dreams, and not in a one-night-stand sort of way, but in a true friendship and deep love way.

When men started paying attention to her blog posts and videos she was putting out there, some of them came to her and said, "I like what you're doing. You really 'get' us men and how we think. Would you help ME find my perfect relationship too?"

At first, she thought, "Of course not, I help women." But then after more than a few men came to her, she decided she *would* most certainly help guys too. Why not?

That's an instance of where niching down created such great content that a whole other group of people who needed her help formed a new market for her. And she didn't even realize it.

That's what I mean when I say people you're not marketing to will find out about you and want to be one of your followers and customers.

Second, people "get it" easier when you tell them what you do if you're specialized. You stick in their minds easier. For example, you're a coach to teenage girls. Or you sell dancewear for ballet and tap dancers who are students and professionals. Or you consult with professional service providers—doctors and lawyers—on marketing.

You're making it very clear to people what you do and who you help. And they can see very easily how you could be the perfect person to solve their problems.

Third, it's easier to do joint ventures or have affiliate partners if your expertise is focused. A joint venture is just that—you partner with someone whose market is your market. Because you're not doing everything, which might seem like you're infringing on "their territory," you come across to them as someone who could help their clients with a problem they don't solve.

Joint venture projects and affiliate partnerships, in which you give affiliate members a percentage of sales they bring to you, are great ways to grow your customer base with people whose clients also need your services. You get to share in each other's list of interested people.

For example, if you're a coach and you work with teenage girls, you can partner with organizations dedicated to teenagers, teen magazines, cosmetics companies and salons, schools and clubs. The possibilities are endless really. It's much easier to promote yourself when you're a specialized coach, rather than being simply "a coach."

Fourth, and this is a big one, people who specialize make more money. When your area of expertise is narrowed in this way, you can charge more money. Generalists are a dime a dozen. And because of the law of supply and demand, if there's a larger supply, the price goes down. You always end up competing on price. But if you specialize, you're one of the gems.

Think about it. A surgeon earns more than a general practice doctor. A root canal specialist earns far more than a dentist. A commercial interior designer earns more than an interior designer.

If someone's looking for a particular provider—let's say a marketing consultant, and there's a choice between a general consultant or one who specializes in their field, there really is no choice. The specialist wins all the time. Plus, the people you don't want to work with won't call you. It's a total win-win situation.

Examples of Narrowing
Here are some examples of narrowing your area of expertise:
- ❖ Dentist vs. a children's dentist
- ❖ Clothing store vs. a men's clothing store or a workman's clothing store
- ❖ Salon vs. a women's salon or an Aveda® women's salon
- ❖ Fitness trainer vs. a women athlete's fitness trainer
- ❖ Nutritionist vs. a holistic gluten-free nutritionist

Also pay attention to this secret you can take advantage of if you specialize: Sometimes it's good to narrow your expertise so you can gain entry to a target market. Then, if you do offer a wider range of help or products, you can reveal them when you're ready and when the customer is ready.

For example, say you're a business coach. That's very broad. But if you specialize in helping corporate people make the jump into owning and running their own business, you can state that's your area of expertise.

But the truth is, you're also knowledgeable about *all* areas of business. So, when your new clients see how great you are at what you do, you might offer them an entire program in how to run a business, which is much more than simply helping them make that transition from corporate to entrepreneurship.

People who were never in the corporate world might want that knowledge from you, too. So even though your specialty is "from corporate to owning your own business," you get to reach many more people by using your specialization as a gateway to you.

How to Narrow Your Area of Expertise

Whether you already have your own business or not, there are a few good ways to really hone in on what your area of expertise might become.

First, if you already own your own business, you've got a start—you know what you do. If you don't know for sure what you want to do, this will help you, too.

Dream. Dream big! Think about all the things you'd really like to do in your business. If you're like most entrepreneurs, you'll come up with more ideas than one person could possibly do.

And the truth is, it doesn't matter which one you choose. Just choose one. Let's say you choose photography. Or you're already a photographer. Just begin thinking about that.

So how do you narrow your expertise?
Are you a pet photographer? A wedding photographer? A children's photographer? A glamour photographer? A portrait photographer? A sports photographer? You may already know if you want to specialize, or you may already be specialized in one of these areas.

If not, again, just choose one. What really makes your heart sing?

Second, look at the numbers. Whatever you choose, do some research. Look on amazon.com to see how many books there are on the topic. Are there a lot? Good. That means there's an interest, which translates into people who'll pay to learn or to get help. Your topic could be photography. But it also could be business coaching, home repair, web design, cooking, interior design, digital marketing. Or whatever you do or dream of doing.

If there aren't very many books and magazines out there, that's not a good thing. Remember, you don't want to invent the wheel. You want to ride on the popularity of interest in a topic.

Go to a newsstand or a big bookstore. See how many magazines there are on the topic. Again, if there are a lot, that's a good thing. It's what people are interested in.

Go into forums of people already doing what you want to do as well as their blog posts. Also go to forums addressing your topic or issues related to it. See what people are asking questions about. Can you help with what they're asking? If so, that's an excellent sign your idea could work.

Here's the secret sauce: Do a web search to see how many people are looking for the topic you're considering. Go to Google keyword research (it's a very long URL, but you can find it by searching in Google for "Google keyword research").
Then see how many searches are conducted on that topic. FYI, on this site, "local" means US searches, which is a good thing for you to know—it's not local, meaning "just down the street." And the number given is the number of searches per month.

What you're looking for is a large number of searches—keep in mind, this is actually what people are searching for, not what you *think* people are searching for—with a much smaller number of sites as an answer to their problem. If you find a phrase or idea with a lot of searches and a very high number of sites, yours will be just one of the crowd.

This research will show you whether there's a Sweet Spot between what you want to do, or what you're already doing, and the demand for it.

What's the Sweet Spot?

Draw a circle to represent what you do or want to do. Draw another circle that intersects the first circle. This second circle represents the demand out there. Where they intersect is known as the Sweet Spot. And the Sweet Spot is where your business will prosper.

It's the intersection of your idea and their solution.

The **third step** is to dream. Yes, dream.

Dream about everything you could offer in your area. If you're a children's photographer, you might think of these ideas:

- ❖ Photograph kids with their favorite costume on and you supply the costumes—a princess, a clown, a superhero, a celebrity.
- ❖ Specialize in taking kids' photos at the local amusement park where you get shots of kids on the merry-go-round or the bumper cars.

> Remember, you don't have to know *everything* about your topic. You just have to know more than the people who are searching for answers. If you know more than they do, you're already the expert to them.

- ❖ Specialize in taking pictures of kids with their favorite stuffed animals or hobby (playing the piano, riding horses, playing soccer).

Consider unorthodox ways of doing your business. Think differently from what other photographers do.

Then decide on a few and add them to your list of "here's how I work" on your website.

That's YOUR Sweet Spot.

What if you already have a business but you want to narrow your area of expertise? How do you tell your current clients?

You can either tell them you're going to start specializing and refer the ones outside your new area of specialization to other practitioners. Or you could still keep your current clients (at least the ones you love working with) and just not take any new ones who are outside your new area of expertise.

Now Go Tell Everyone

You've done a lot of work here to make some amazing decisions that will clearly advance your business.

Now it's time to let everyone know!

Make sure these parts of your marketing include exactly what you do in a very obvious way: your website, your business card, your signature in your email, your bio that is on articles you write, or that gets read out loud before any presentations you give, and your profiles on all social media.

Make a freebie for you to give away on your website (a recommended way to get new people to sign up for your email— they're told they'll be hearing from you when they sign up for the freebie). Your freebie directly addresses something about your specialty.

For example, going back to the photographer example, your freebie could be "7 Tips on How to Get Your Child to Look Her Best in Front of the Camera." Or, "5 Must-Do's Before You Get Your Next Professional Photo so You Look Amazing."

Write as the expert. Be the expert you are.

Be sure to include this freebie on the back of your business card. Then when you meet someone and they express interest in what you do, hand them your card and say, "I have a great tip sheet about this exact thing. You can go here to download it."

And you never have to "sell" anyone on you and what you do. You can just be yourself and you'll sell yourself. Not so hard to do.

Remember, when you include your bio for any articles you write, *not* to link people to your home page on your website. Instead link them to your opt-in page for your freebie. Your bio would say something like, "June Doe is a children's photographer who specializes in photographing kids doing their favorite things. To find out how to get your child to look her best, go here to download a free tip sheet." And include your link to it.

You're all set up now to go into your new narrowed area of specialization.

We've talked about why it's important for you to narrow your area of expertise—to reach more people, to make alliances easier, and to earn more money. We've also talked about examples of narrowing from one specialization to something even more "special." And we've talked about exactly how you can go about doing the process of finding your own niche through dreaming, research and deciding. Finally, we talked about how to let everyone know about your new niche through all your marketing, as well as when you're talking to people.

I just know you'll be a firehouse of power in your newly defined niche.

Now go out there and be the unstoppable entrepreneur you were meant to be!

Jennifer "Jenny" Engle, an award winning marketing and communications professional and entrepreneur, is a popular speaker, trainer, and author. As the owner and principal of jke marketing & communications, she is active in the for- and not-for-profit sectors. Her business, which is Green Plus Certified, focuses on incorporating sustainable practices into everyday operations.

One of Pennsylvania's top 50 Women in Business and Central PA's 25 Women of Influence, Jenny is a platinum level member of WomenCentric Speakers Bureau, a trainer with MVP Seminars, an expert with Problem Solved Daily, and the past national president of the Association for Women in Communications.

In addition to being a contributing author to this book, Jenny is a featured chapter author in <u>The Unstoppable Woman's Guide to Emotional Wellbeing</u>, as well as a featured contributor to the *PRNEWS Employee Communications Handbook, the PRNEWS Guidebook on CSR and Green Messaging* and the *2012 Women's Advantage Calendar*. She enjoys social media and regularly blogs and writes on communicating professionally, perfecting your writing skills, being your own cheerleader, building positive professional relationships, and strategic planning and positioning.

A strong believer in lifelong learning, Jenny earned an MPA from Penn State University and a BS from Millersville University. This "Unstoppable Woman" enjoys giving back and is a mentor to many young women, volunteers actively in her community, and serves on numerous boards.

Jennifer K. Engle
jke marketing & communications
1845 Brubaker Run Rd. Lancaster, PA 17603
717-295-1685
jkengle2@aol.com
www.jkecommunications.com

Chapter 5

Building a Top Quality Team
Jennifer K. Engle

Building a team for your new venture is a daunting task, but it can make all the difference between future success and failure. Like marriage, hiring employees, whether they are subcontractors or permanent, should not be entered into lightly! The key to achieving your goals is making sure you work with the right players. How do you begin the process of finding these colleagues with whom you may be spending a good part of your life?

Assessing Your Needs

- **Does your business really need employees?**

To answer this question, you'll need to look at your business and strategic plans. Can you succeed as a sole proprietor—at least for a while? Do you really need to hire someone or should you outsource? This decision usually boils down to identifying your main areas of strength and how often certain skills are needed. Many times subcontractors have more skills and experience than you can realistically afford to hire.

- **Where does your workload stand?**

Is it steady? Growing? Feast or famine? Obviously, you should have at least 12 to 16 months of confirmed work before you even think about hiring an employee. If you're going gangbusters and can project an ongoing, strong workload, sit down and take a good, hard look at your anticipated needs in staffing. Prioritize each growth position and create a rough timeline for hiring.

Are you overwhelmed with certain aspects of the workload? Perhaps you only need someone to help with a particular project or for a certain period of time. Think about a freelancer or two.

- **Are you operating profitably?**

Carefully analyze your budget to determine if you have the flexibility to hire someone. If your cash flow is precarious or your clients do not pay promptly, you may want to reconsider. Remember, you don't have to hire a permanent employee or even a full-time employee at first. Perhaps hiring a subcontractor or freelancer would be the better option.

- **What does your timeline look like?**

Remember that you are not just your company's HR manager— you also are doing a ton of work on a daily basis. The hiring process can take months. Unless you're extremely fortunate, good people don't just pop up. So, plan ahead. Although you may not want to do this and it may not be your strong suit, you'll find the process much less painful and intimidating if you don't wait until you *really* need someone to begin the hunt.

If you procrastinate, you're going to end up frustrated, behind the eight ball, and continuing to work for months *really* needing someone.

The Next Milestone

Whether your response to the above questions is hiring subcontractors or employees, you're ready to face your next milestone.

Which is…in addition to being your own boss, you're now going to be someone else's! More than likely, you'll face this task—being a recruiter, interviewer, negotiator, and possibly, a lawyer—by yourself. Scary, huh? But, don't worry, according to Seth Godin and Gloria Steinem, fear is a sign of growth. It means you are stretching and moving outside your comfort zone. After all, you wouldn't have become an entrepreneur if you were adamantly opposed to reasonable risk taking.

Whether you decide to go with the subcontractor or employee route, there are a variety of aspects you'll want to consider when building your team. Personally, I spent just as much time selecting my team of subcontractors as many of my colleagues did on hiring regular employees. Only you can decide which are most important in the short and long runs, but you should decide up front what compromises and/or trade-offs you may be willing to make.

Be prepared to make more compromises if the rates or salary you can offer are on the lower end of the scale. Remember how you felt during interviews when organizations gave you job descriptions four pages long? Many also wanted at least ten years of experience and a variety of top-tier qualifications, only to offer a salary comparable to what you earned ten years ago. So, be realistic and fair. Be sure to check with your attorney on specific contract, hiring and firing, and compensation issues and brush up on proper interviewing procedures.

Finding the Talent

Outside of hiring people from a past employer, networking is one of the best ways for an entrepreneur to find potential employees. Specifically ask for referrals from friends, industry colleagues, fellow board members, your accountant or attorney, or members of professional and civic organizations. Not only does this method eliminate the hundreds of résumés you may get by posting positions online via Monster or Career Builder, but it also cuts down on screening time.

You also may want to consider asking members of particular professional LinkedIn groups to which you belong. If you've been blogging or posting regularly in Google Plus circles or Facebook, you may have already received queries from interested individuals. These are the typical methods start-ups and smaller businesses use to find their initial employees.

After you hire someone, don't forget to ask him or her for referrals. Studies show this method has high success rates, most likely because employees will normally only recommend someone they feel confident would do well at the company. No one wants to tarnish his reputation with a poor recommendation. If you must look elsewhere, consider niche online job boards, local newspapers, or trade groups and professional organizations' websites.

Screening and Interviewing

Forget the gimmicks and big company rule books; here are some smart tips for finding a great hire. Also, included is a sample checklist of questions which you may adapt to your specific needs:

1. **Hire someone who shares your values and "gets" or blends with your overall personality.**

   A great way to determine whether someone can potentially put up with working long hours with you is to incorporate your character and beliefs into the project or job description. Be humorous, creative, or detailed-oriented (depending on your personality as well as the position being offered), and clearly signal the individuality of your company.

   Here are a few examples:

   Values: We demonstrate our honesty and integrity by sharing our strengths and weaknesses, taking reasonable risks and delivering on promises.

   Looking for a great writer: We're looking for someone who thinks writing great copy is like creating a super duper sundae and enjoying it—even through the brain freeze!

   Customer service skills: We're looking for someone who can jump into our customers' shoes (literally) and anticipate their needs and concerns.

In today's job market, your ad posting can generate hundreds or thousands of responses. If you receive generic, run of the mill rhetoric in cover letters, chuck them (but first, generate an email "thank you for applying" message and let them know that you will follow up within two weeks if you have further interest). On the other hand, if you receive responses that reflect and play off of your descriptions, you've found potential partners. To further narrow the candidate pool, consider asking applicants to write a few paragraphs on a small number of topics. You might want to write something like this:

"Thank you for your résumé and cover letter. The next step in our hiring process involves writing a maximum of three paragraphs on three of the topics below. You may choose to respond to any three questions." Offer a deadline and directions to those who apply.

Sample questions:

- o *Why would you like to work with XYZ Company?*
- o *How long are you willing to keep pushing on a good project until you give up and why?*
- o *How hard is it to get you to change your mind when you're wrong?*
- o *Describe a situation in your work or home life where you failed. What did you learn?*
- o *How long does it take you to learn something new?*
- o *Describe something you accomplished that you thought was impossible.*

What will happen at this point? Usually, only serious candidates will respond. Not only will you learn if they can communicate clearly and succinctly, but you also will discover what type of work ethic they have and if they fit with your culture. Another plus is that you'll have interesting topics for interviews.

I recommend keeping the contact information for these "interested" candidates. They can have many benefits, including members of future focus groups, future employees, tweeters on various subjects, etc. Depending upon the business nature of your company, you may want to give them a discount coupon, a voucher for a small product, or an invitation to download a free e-book, white paper or video. This is such an unusual practice, I'm sure many of them will share via social media. *Never miss an opportunity to generate good will and brand awareness!*

2. **Look for people with strengths that complement yours and/or fill in the deficits**.

Although you want candidates who share your values, you don't necessarily want team members who are too similar to you, whether that means Boomers or Gen Xers or perhaps a group of creative, hard working, curious types. In reality, you need players of diverse types to make your business successful. This includes individuals of varying age and experience levels as well as those of different ethnic backgrounds and personality types. Do your best to ensure that each person's skills complement, but do not overshadow one another. Often, hiring someone who has strong leadership traits but is accustomed to working solo may create friction in a team-oriented environment. Conversely, if you have a group of young, creative workers who lack organization and attention to detail, you may want to seek out a more mature person who possesses these talents and can keep these guys on track without intimidating them or dampening their enthusiasm.

3. **Hire someone who has a "smaller business" mentality.**

While it may be appealing to hire a person with impressive big-business credentials, he or she probably will not be a good fit. Your company is definitely not Microsoft, Deloitte Touche, or Johnson & Johnson. An individual from those kinds of large organizations is used to rules, regulations, and bureaucracy. In addition, he or she may have had assistants and technical help. Most likely, you are looking for someone who can work with minimal supervision and hand-holding. In your company, there may be no particular procedures, no set jobs, and everyone will need to step up and fill in when necessary. Flexibility is key, as is a desire to learn, improve, or enhance skill sets. In addition, since you are a small operation, individuals must be willing to put in the extra hours when necessary.

4. Scrutinize resumes carefully!

Everyone has different viewpoints on résumés, but I have found that a person can look really good on paper and be a dud when it comes to performance. Much information can be faked or exaggerated. Certainly, you need to know that someone has the basic skills, knowledge, and experience you need, but there is no way to tell if they are right for you unless you talk with them. If someone were to look at your résumé, would they think you were experienced enough to start a business? Perhaps not, but you did it anyway. Often, traits such as perseverance, determination, and motivation can be more important than fabulous degrees or big awards. That being said, be cautious of "superstars." Use the résumé as a starting point—not the be-all/end-all—for conversations and trust your gut instincts.

5. **Require good communication skills!**

No matter what position you are seeking to fill, your new colleague(s) need(s) to be able to communicate clearly and correctly—verbally and in writing. In small businesses, there are no layers separating employees from employees and/or employees from customers. Everyone talks to each other. Everyone will write to each other. Everyone may, in fact, write blog entries, tweet, make entries on Facebook and Google Plus, or write and appear in videos. It's important that each team member be able to handle themselves confidently in a variety of situations. Responses to questions during the screening process (mentioned in #1), as well as interview conversations should serve as prime indicators of these skills or the potential to improve or enhance these skills. Again, trust your gut.

6. **Be prepared to create a positive work environment.**

Think back to the reasons you wanted to strike out on your own. Were feeling unappreciated or working in a negative environment among your main motives? Keep those thoughts in mind as you build your organization. You've been working solo for awhile now, and you may have forgotten how to say "thank you" or "good job" to others. When you are building a top quality team, you want to be sure to let them know their services are valued, that their work helps to grow the success of the business. When you have a culture that exemplifies your mission, vision and values and you treat your team with dignity and respect, they will give their best.

7. Include phone and in-person interviews in the screening process.

The rationale for using multiple screening options is that you are able to see and hear how an applicant performs in a variety of circumstances and situations—just as they would in your work place. Since the candidate has passed the written communication stage, you'll want to learn if he or she does equally well in other areas. A phone interview has its pros and cons, but it will allow you to discover if an individual can speak clearly and professionally and if he or she is prepared and understands how to convince you to want to learn more. Although you won't be able to see posture, body language, and facial expressions, you will be able to experience how clients might feel when talking with this person. You may even want to ask the applicant to role play with you or talk via Skype.

By the time you get to the in-person interview, you should have a good general impression of the candidate. As you query that person on the details of a résumé or ask for elaboration on experience and potential reactions to work situations, you should monitor the nonverbal cues. How comfortable does he seem? Is she calm and well prepared? Is she taking notes? Is he arrogant or a show boater?

☐ **Appearance**	
☐ **Communication skills**	
☐ **Demeanor**	
☐ **Eye contact**	
☐ **Confidence**	
☐ **Taking notes?**	
☐ **Asks questions**	
☐ **Knows company info**	
☐ **Strengths**	
☐ **Weaknesses or limitations**	

Making the Hire & Keeping Your Eye On The Ball

So, you have come to a decision and made an offer of employment and/or offered a contractual agreement to a subcontractor. Remember the characteristics you have always appreciated in a boss and keep them in mind as you go about your daily operations. In addition, give the new team members adequate orientation and training or direction, regardless of what you choose to call it. Time spent up front making sure expectations and operations are clear is always time well spent.

Finally, your strategic plans may change as your business evolves and grows. So, too, may your team. The skills you need now may not be the same ones you need in a few years. Regularly re-evaluate your team to get the greatest value and best results. The formula for your business success may involve retraining, realigning, additional hiring, or even terminating, but the best way to build a top-quality team is to give the process the attention it deserves.

Luz N. Adams, RN, BSN, MS, CMC Luz is an accomplished, articulate Nurse Clinical Educator, Master Coach, Published Author, Motivational Speaker, Instructor and Counselor, Health Advocate, Consultant and Registered Nurse with 30 years of success as a "driving force' in healthcare and health education, meeting challenges, setting standards and generating improvements through system changes and training.

Luz is also a Reiki Master, a Clinical Hypnotherapist, a Past Life Regression Therapist, and a Spiritual Instructor (Free Soul Organization). She holds certifications as a Health and Wellness Coach, Spiritual Coach, NLP Coach, Group Coach, Life Coach and Master Coach. She has created workshops, classes, and retreats for health care providers and the general public.

Luz is the president and owner of Integrated Holistic Concepts. Her success is built on the ability to inspire teamwork and tap into the unique expertise of others. She is uniquely qualified to present a continuum of information from traditional medicine to holistic healing that provides people the choices to include more self-care and wellness in their lives. As her life experiences sit at the crossroads of traditional medicine and holistic wellness with 30 years of experience as a highly credentialed nurse, and over 25 years of spirituality experience and teaching, she can see both sides: the worldly and the spiritual. She acts as the interpreter and guide for both approaches to wellness by explaining the terrain and presenting choices for people. She knows and loves what she does.

Contact Information:
Luz@IntegratedHolisticConcepts.com
www.IntegratedHolisticConcepts.com

Chapter 6

Becoming Known as an Expert
Luz Adams

This chapter will concentrate on the process of becoming an expert so you can use your expertise, knowledge, and experience to successfully grow your business or enterprise. To prepare for this chapter, I conducted a survey and asked people two questions: "What is an expert?", and "What makes someone an expert?" The answers are varied, however, there were four themes that came in quite strong: **Knowledge, Skills, Analyzing, and Sharing.** It also showed me that there are two words that seem to be interchangeable when you talk about being an expert: Expert and Expertise. So let's start by defining an expert.

What is an expert?
An expert is a person that is recognized as a reliable source; someone with advanced knowledge and/or a mastery of skills in a particular topic, field, industry or domain that can analyze a situation and who is willing to share that knowledge and skill with others. A person is considered an expert because of his or her extensive knowledge or skills based on education, research or experience in a particular field or industry. It can also be someone perceived to have more knowledge in a subject or industry than the average person. Experts also have the ability to influence others due to their knowledge or skills.

The term expert is used to describe professionals such as medical doctors, dentists, PhD's, accountants, physicists, chemists, teachers, and scientists. But the field also includes any individual that has attained superior performance by instruction or practice such as artists, musicians, painters, writers, speakers, or athletes. Experts tend to exhibit their superior performance and skills in a way that appears effortless. They make it look easy.

> *"Never become so much of an expert that you stop gaining expertise. View life as a continuous learning experience."*
> -Denis Waitley

What is expertise?

Expertise is the skill of an expert; the knowledge that distinguishes a person in a field or a domain from less experienced people. An expert uses his expertise and ability to recognize the problem in a situation. An expert is able to diagnose it, knows the answer to the problem, or knows a way to solve the problem and then is able to solve the problem and share the solutions with others. Expertise is developed with experience, knowledge, and time. Experts are believers in "Life Long Learning."

> *"Some will know less, some will know more;*
> *Be an expert to those who know less,*
> *Learn from those who know more."*
> -   Luz Adams

Why do you want to become an expert?

There are many reasons why you want to become an expert. Let's explore some of them.

> Becoming an expert will **establish credibility** for you, your business, and your product.

> Become and expert so that other people will seek you out for information, products, advice, and **for the knowledge** you have to share with them. Show your clients that you know a lot about your niche. Being an expert makes you the go-to person in your business and your industry.

> Experts always continue to learn, explore, find new ways of doing things, identify new patterns, apply new solutions and share their expertise with others. Help others **find the solutions and resolve** their problems and they will continue to seek you out.

> Being known as an expert will **create a powerful platform** for your career or business.

> Being an expert will **expand your horizons** and will help you look at the world in a different way. You will always be looking for solutions and ways to solve problems in a different and unique way.

> Becoming an expert will help you **attain success** by focusing on what you can improve.

> Becoming an expert will help you gain **the trust** of others. Once you have their trust, they will seek you out for your knowledge, your expertise, and to connect with you.

> Becoming an expert, will help you establish yourself as an industry **leader**. Help others by becoming a trusted resource so that you will be asked to do interviews, get exposure through various media outlets, gain access to conferences, land speaking engagements, and receive

networking invitations. Becoming an expert will allow you to convert followers into customers and sales.

"An investment in knowledge always pays the best interest"
Ben Franklin

How do you become an Expert?

We've reviewed both the words "expert" and "expertise" and we understand that experts are knowledgeable, skillful analyzers, and enjoy sharing with others their expertise, which is their skill and ability. So how do you become an expert? Gain expertise to become an expert in your business, your product, your profession, or your niche. An example would be a travel agent. Travel agents can sell airline tickets, vacations, cruises, and destination packages. There is a lot a travel agent can do for you, but if you wanted to take a safari in Africa, or explore the Mayan ruins, or visit Disney World wouldn't you want to use a travel agent that specializes in those areas? Travel agents choose a niche such as cruises, Disney destinations, honeymoon vacations, or adventure travel.

Let's suppose you are planning a honeymoon or you have three kids who want to see Disney World. There are Disney specialists (experts) that could tell you about all the features of Disney. They know all the insider secrets, tricks and tips to get the most out of your vacation.

The expert will focus on the areas at Disney that would be more appropriate for each member of the family. The honeymooners might want romantic candlelight dinners, a couple's massage, a quiet hotel. The kids would want to know the exciting rides, having breakfast with Mickey and Minnie, staying in a Disney theme hotel with lots of activities and other children to play with. The Disney travel agent specialist would know how to create a vacation where each family member gets the perfect and most memorable visit. This is how experts position themselves above the competition to be the best choice for your travel agent.

To become an expert you need to do your homework. You want to earn credentials, get some real world experience, continue your industry related education, stay on top of trends, keep up to date, check your industry websites, subscribe to trade journals and publications, become a member of trade associations and attend conventions and meetings. Read books, listen to books on tape, watch other people's videos, and learn from other experts. It will not happen overnight, but you can become an expert by preparing and learning. Make "Life Long Learning" your motto. Never stop learning and acquiring more knowledge.

Do not stop sharing and giving to others. No matter how much you think you know, there is always more to learn. There are more ideas and content, new skills, new shifts, and new people from whom to learn. The world is changing constantly. There will always be new ideas, new gadgets, new products, and new ways of doing things. Increase your knowledge to a slightly higher level than the average person. Challenge yourself to learn more by setting specific goals, use SMART goals (**S**pecific, **M**easurable, **A**ttainable, **R**ealistic and **T**imely). Seek opportunities that provide growth and progress to develop expertise in your business.

What are some of the actions you need to do to become an expert and to demonstrate your expertise? Let's explore some ideas.

Networking

If you want to grow your business, people need to know that you exist. You need to find people and share your story with them. People love to hear stories and also love to talk about themselves. Ask *them* questions, find out *their* dreams, find out what makes *them* happy, find out what keeps *them* up at night, find out what problems *they* have that *they* would love to solve. If you have a solution let them know. If you do not, but you know someone else that does, refer them. A perfect example of this was reflected in the classic movie, "Miracle on 34th St" when the employees at Macy's were referring customers to Kimball's and Macy's proceeded to increase their sales.

Take time to build your foundation and your experience before you put on your expert hat. Benefit from third party validation and let others call you or refer to you as an expert. It increases your credibility. Otherwise, you could open yourself to criticism and scrutinizing of your credentials. Instead, promote yourself as a specialist or an experienced person and let others call you the expert.

Writing

Here are some easy and inexpensive ways to get others to know you and your business. You can publish:

- ❖ Press releases
- ❖ Newsletters
- ❖ Blogs
- ❖ Articles
- ❖ e-zines
- ❖ e-books
- ❖ Books

Give your opinion and invite others to ask questions. Ask what problems need to be solved, what people worry about, what keeps them up at night, what would make them happier, healthier, wealthier, and more peaceful. Listen to what others want and be prepared to provide solutions, results, or resources.

Create your own web page and/or blog. Share information, write white papers, and market your own e-zine, e-book or book. With the power of self publishing using Amazon, Barnes and Noble, and others, it is a lot easier to write and publish your own material now. Writing and publishing is a great foundation to build your career and your business. You can be recognized as an expert in one or many areas. Once you have written your books and e-books, market them on your website. They can serve as catalyst for creating speaking engagements and interviews.

One of the most effective ways of being a trusted advisor is to give away your material for free. People are more likely to open their wallets, when you open your heart. It's a myth that if you give away your best information, that the public won't need you anymore. Quite the contrary; people will feel like they can't live without you because you have provided them with value at no cost. You can provide press clippings and articles to give-away and stay fresh in your customer's mind.

Social Media

The world has become a very small place with the use of the internet, e-mail, Facebook, LinkedIn, and Twitter. The same way you use your blogs, use social media to share your information, ask questions, and suggest solutions and provide results. You can ask questions and get advice or someone can ask a question and be the expert by giving advice.   By providing good free advice that provides real value, you will build a base of fans that trust you and will seek out your expertise.

Through word-of-mouth, others start talking about you and recommend you to their friends. How many times have you watched a movie or read a good book and you can't wait to tell your friends and co-workers about it? The same thing will happen with your business. Tell everyone what you do and what services you provide, but most importantly, tell them what **results** you offer.

Ask for testimonials and place them on your webpage and your social media site. LinkedIn and BranchOut have areas for endorsements. Give endorsements and ask for endorsements from your network of friends and customers.

Education

Education is important for your own growth and expertise. Seek out new information and knowledge. With all the technology available now, it is easy to market your business and show people what you know. Creating on-line courses, webinars, classes, and workshops help you establish yourself as an expert in a topic or area of interest while generating revenue. Use MeetMe.com, Gotomeeting.com, and WebEx.com to create presentations. From your home or at your office, you can offer your clients the same benefit and make it easy to attend your event without leaving the comfort of their home or office. This is a great way to build your business nationwide or worldwide without the travel time and expense.

Use classes to grow your business, offer free webinars and how-to classes. Then advertise other products or up sale another line of products or solutions with your offer. After your class or seminar, convert your students into leads and add them to your data base. Let them know when you have new classes or products, and invite them to attend using an incentive. Ask them for referrals, anecdotes, testimonials and references to use in your Website.

Videos

Create your own videos and offer your own YouTube channel. If you do not know how to create a YouTube video, YouTube.com has instructions that will guide you step by step on how to create and publish your video. From your own channel, gather friends and followers that you can place in your database and convert to paying clients. If you do not feel comfortable getting in front of the camera, create Power Point presentations and show them in your video as you speak and explain them. Talk about something where you know more than the average person or that covers an area of interest to others. People are always searching for how-to's and advice. If you are not camera shy, then step in front of the camera as people like to *see* the expert. It will give you credibility and establish rapport and trust with your potential clients. Do not forget to add your videos to your website. Remember those classes we talked about earlier? They can be taped. Later, market them as a product or place them on your website or get them transcribed and use them as e-books, e-zines, or white papers. Always think of ways to turn your material into products that you can sell or give away as incentives to build your business.

Speaking Engagements

While it is very difficult for many people to speak in front of groups (public speaking is one of people's greatest fears) it is a great way to become known as an expert. If you need some practice, attend a Toastmasters group in your area and learn to speak comfortably in front of audiences.

Many groups and associations are always looking for speakers for their monthly meetings. Register yourself with Speaker's Bureaus in your area. Depending on your expertise and the topics you present, you can market yourself during these speaking engagements. Sell your products to create an additional source of income. Advertise on your website or blog that you are a speaker and ask to be invited to speak about your area of expertise.

Attend seminars, workshops, industry conferences, trade shows, associations, Chamber of Commerce meetings and networking events. Let everyone know that you have a business, carry business cards, and practice your 30 second elevator speech to talk about your brand. You are the person in charge of promoting yourself. When someone asks you, "What do you do?" be prepared to give them your 30 second elevator speech. There are only three things you need in your 30 second speech: 1. What your specialty is, 2. who your target market is, 3. what benefit or result they will receive. Once you answer those questions and refine your statement, memorize it and practice it! Use word-of-mouth marketing to communicate your expertise and your business.

Consulting

Be willing to offer consultations and counseling services. Depending on your product or business, to gain more experience, you can offer your consulting services pro-bono (no charge) to shelters, churches, and organizations. It will help you establish yourself as an expert, build your list of credentials and it shows that you are willing to share. Ask for referrals and recommendations of others needing your expertise. Your goal is always to offer your services to generate business income. Offering a free 15 minute consultation or speaking to non-profit groups is a great way to get exposure for your business.

Interviews

Promote yourself and your book with interviews. Seek out opportunities to speak and write or talk about your topic, your business and your niche to the public. The bigger the forum, the more exposure you create.

Radio, newspapers, and television are good sources for interviews. Call a radio, newspaper, or local television station and offer to be interviewed on a unique product, your new book, or a topic of interest to a particular audience that relates to your business. Another way to get interviews is to use Press Releases. Send them to the local radio and television stations or newspapers. Editors are always looking for new and fresh material of interest to their audiences. This will get you more exposure.

Many Public Access (radio and television) stations offer classes to become a radio or television producer. Take the class and then create your own show. Usually the shows are co-owned by both the station and the show's producer for a period of time and then released back to the producer. Once your program is released back to you, send your programs to other similar stations to be aired. It is called "bicycling" your show. This will create even more exposure for you as the "expert" and for your business.

"Go confidently in the direction of your dreams.
Live the life you have imagined."
Henry David Thoreau

What's next?

We have looked at what an expert and having expertise is. We have examined the benefits of becoming an expert. We explored how to gain expertise by networking, writing, public speaking and giving interviews, by using social media and videos, by consulting and through further education. Now that you know how to become an expert, what do you do next?

First, **Believe in Yourself.** When you project confidence others will feel it too. They will seek your advice and will want to know how you do it. No matter what you do, always give it your best, act with integrity, and provide 110% value to your customers. An expert exceeds client's expectations.

Second, **Be Original**. Find your own way of doing things and learn to shine in your field. Separate yourself from the competition, offer something unique, different and with a twist. Do everything with passion, feel your passion and let it be your guide.

Third, **Show You Care**. Remember the saying "It's not how much you know - it's how much you care." Being an expert is more than just who you are or what you do; it is the results you deliver that really matter to your customers. As an expert, provide a "Wow" experience for your customers, from the heart.

Finally, **TAKE ACTION!** Set goals. Learn, acquire knowledge, gain skills and share with people. Create a plan to incorporate all these suggestions and integrate the ones that especially resonate with you into a campaign to develop expertise in your field.

Become an expert in your business, and like spokes on the wheel, market in all directions to grow. In your journey to become an expert and a successful entrepreneur, help everyone you meet to become … Unstoppable!

Major (P) Alexis (Lex) Neal, US Army Infantry

Recently selected for promotion to Lieutenant Colonel, Alexis Neal is an Infantry Officer in the United States Army. He is a well-traveled Army officer with multiple deployments to Afghanistan, Iraq, Bosnia, and Kosovo. He was responsible for planning and executing some of the largest and most effective operations throughout Baghdad and southern Iraq, as well as Paktika, Helmand, and Kandarhar provinces in Afghanistan.

As a military strategist and operational planner, Major Neal assisted in the implementation of multiple small and medium businesses in theatres.

Lex received his Bachelor's of Arts and Science in Architectural Studies from the University of Arkansas; Master's in Business and Security Management from Webster University; and Master's in Military Arts and Science from the U.S. Army's Command and General Staff College. He is also a graduate of the Army's School of Advanced Military Studies, where he specialized in planning, designing, and operating in complex environments. His military awards consist of two Bronze Stars, a Defense Meritorious Service Medal, four Meritorious Service Medals, two Army Commendation Medals, two Army Achievement Medals, an Army Reserve Commendation Medal, two National Defense Service Medals, an Armed Forces Expeditionary Medal, an Army Superior Unit Award, a German Armed Forces Badge for Weapons Proficiency, two Afghanistan Campaign Medals for Combat Service, a Global War on Terror Expeditionary Medal, a Global War on Terror Service Medal, an Armed Forces Service Medal, an Army Service Ribbon, six Overseas Service Ribbons, a NATO Defense Medal, an Army Parachutist Badge, a US Army Ranger Badge, an Expert Infantryman Badge, and the coveted Combat Infantryman's Badge. Lex is married to Sylvia Hauser and has one daughter, Nele.

Chapter 7

Planning & Executing

Major Alexis Neal

After spending more than two decades in the US Army, I have learned some very effective ways of planning and executing operations. The most important factor that determines the success of a plan is first identifying what it is that you are attempting to accomplish; this is your mission statement. Once you achieve a clear understanding of the mission, establish your objectives then develop measures or indicators to determine if and how well you are succeeding in accomplishing your short- and long-term objectives. Throughout the execution of a business plan, conduct periodic assessments; if it becomes necessary, adjust that plan and make course corrections to avoid shocks and predict business success. For a complicated or complex problem, a good business plan starts with understanding.

To gain an understanding of your mission, objectives and success indicators, you first need to define the parameters that directly influence mission success for the business. For the purposes of this chapter, we will refer to this as "defining the problem." This forces entrepreneurs to refrain from the cliché of "thinking outside the box," but instead challenges them to *create* their own box or the conditions under which a business will flourish.

These conditions are based on your mission and what you have chosen to accomplish.

Creating Your Box

1. Creating your box is the deliberate process of establishing the physical, economical, and psychological constraints and limitations of the business. The box defines what must and must not be done to guarantee success. **Competition**. Who are the real and perceived competitors who may prevent your business from being successful?
   a. Who is the competition and why?
   b. What are the risks of having competition?
   c. Does your competition expose your vulnerabilities?
   d. How do you reduce your own risks and exploit your competition?

2. **Resources available.** What resources are on hand or can be borrowed?
   a. What are the operational requirements?
   b. What are the emergency and contingency requirements?
   c. What does your current credit rating offer you? What are your credit requirements to maintain a functioning business? What risks will you assume with creditors, and if so, how much? How do you prioritize payments to creditors?
   d. What is your economic tolerance?
   e. What is your initial investment?

3. **Time.** What are the trends that may have positive and negative effects on this business?
   a. How do seasons affect your business?
   b. What are the earning seasons?
   c. When must you start displaying profits to the investors/lenders/benefactors?

4. **Location.** Based on available resources, where can the business achieve the desired results?
   a. What are the physical location requirements?
   b. Does this business exist in cyberspace alone, or is a combination of physical and Internet locations more beneficial?
5. **Environment.** What are the environmental factors that can affect sales or services?
   a. What is the physical, seasonal, spiritual, and political terrain?
   b. How does the environment affect the business?
   c. What are the risks, vulnerabilities, capabilities, and requirements of the environment?

Mission Statement

A clear understanding of the mission determines what services or products you will provide. Effectively, the mission statement takes what is implicit in an entrepreneur's head and makes it explicit for others who are associated with or invested in the business. For example, if you were selling a brand of clothing, your mission statement may look like this:

Best Clothing Company imports quality materials from Southeast Asia and distributes to online retail customers and East Coast wholesalers to turn a 40% profit from invested funds each month.

This mission statement is constructed using the Four W's and the How:

Who: Best Clothing Company
What: Imports and distributes
Where: East Coast

Why: To turn a 40% profit from invested funds
How: Online retail and East Coast wholesalers

This mission statement in conjunction with the five conditions, in which you created your box, sets the foundation for you to develop the plan and envision achievable long- and short-term objectives. As you start answering those five questions, you will start setting the constraints and limitations of your business practices.

Zones of Tolerance

"Zones of tolerance" are the environment, physical, financial, or other personal limitations that you have assessed to fit within your scope of risks—that is, the limits you don't want to exceed. To stay within your identified zones of tolerance, business plan writers should understand seasonal trends and implement measures of learning about the trends and understanding what impact they will have. Measures of learning are the real or perceived actions which provide indicators to business owners that their business is trending in desired or undesirable directions. The measures of learning facilitate owners' capability to visualize trends by looking for those certain indicators before or as they are occurring. These indicators will provide conscious entrepreneur to foresee that their assessed limitations are being approached. Assessments and further analysis will determine what course corrections you must implement. Entrepreneurs must avoid making excessive course corrections in which the outcome cannot be anticipated. An understanding of the business' physical, financial and psychological limitations allows owners to continue to steer the business towards positive trends. If negative trends are realized and the conditions for are establish to mitigate the negative trends, then recovery from the setbacks can also be anticipated.

Business owners must be careful not to extend themselves beyond their constraints and limitations. As the business progresses along positive trajectories, you may desire to revisit your acceptable levels of tolerance. Business owners may wish to increase their levels of acceptable risks to anticipate more profitable successes.

Objectives

The long-term objectives of an organization are envisioned by those who invested into the business. This is how the business owners determine the vision (given the constraints, limitations, and social, economic, and other contributing environmental factors)— by identifying and communicating the realistic objectives of the business. With the understanding of the vision, the planner takes the contributing factors into consideration, projects short-term objectives, and lays out a timeline for those objectives to be reached (see Figure 1).

When carefully developed and analyzed short-term objectives develop a cause-and-effect relationship with the terminal objective. If interim objective 1 is accomplished and if interim objective 2 is accomplished, that provides the necessary conclusion that the terminal objective will also be accomplished. To accomplish the interim objectives, carefully scrutinize the measures of performance, or MOP. The MOP are the real and physical actions that are essential in delivering the decisive effects required to meet the interim objectives. Because MOP are real and physical actions, they are not subject to interpretation as to whether they exist or not. Contrarily, interim objectives are more subjective and based on the entrepreneur's perception; they are open to interpretation.

Consider this example: Marvin's terminal objective is to get hired for a job. He develops the interim objectives of (1) dress to impress; (2) arrive on time; and (3) interview well. The interim objectives are subject to opinion, but lead Marvin to believe that if these three objectives are accomplished, he will in fact get hired for the job.

The MOP are the physical actions required to "dress to impress"—maintaining personal hygiene and dressing in a suit and tie. The physical actions required to arrive on time are waking up, having breakfast, and having his route to the office planned in advance. The MOP for interviewing well may be the physical actions of rehearsing his introduction and preparing answers for anticipated questions, practicing his handshake, and standing upright. Although these actions by themselves don't have an individual cause-and-effect relationship on Marvin being hired, collectively they have more of a positive causality, instilling in Marvin the belief that he will be hired.

Trend Identification

Looking at the problem as a whole and creating your box in which your business should exist and thrive, you can expect the life of the business to resemble a wave which cycles through positive and negative trends. These trends are based on physical, economical, and other environmental factors (see Figure 2). The business will have highs and lows depending on environmental factors in the community and economic markets. Throughout the execution of a business plan, you will look for the indicators that lead you to the valid and necessary deductions to predict or otherwise forecast progress. However, it is the planning phase that provides the analysis to determine what indicators will provide those forecasts of future performances. Previously, I discussed the conditions based upon your mission, in which I suggested that you dispose of the cliché of "thinking outside of the box," and rather create your own box. It is the planner's analysis of these conditions by which he or she ascertains when and where potential opportunities will present themselves. The understanding of environmental changes helps the planner not to be deceived by false indicators.

Also during this analysis is when the business establishes reasonable conditions to exploit seasonal trends. This analysis provides planners the opportunity to mitigate the risks identified with trends of the seasons, market values, suppliers, and customers.

In risk mitigation, you will conduct an analysis to identify when and where risks will present themselves. Once you understand the risks, you will conduct another level of analysis to determine what effect those risks will have on the business and whether the risks can and should be mitigated. If a risk is too high and cannot be mitigated, the planner goes back to the drawing board to determine if this is, in fact, a suitable, feasible, and acceptable business venture.

Consider, for instance, Best Clothing Company, which provides imported Southeast Asian fabrics that are typically used to make beach and summer textiles to markets along the East Coast. BCC expressed some of the following concerns based on its analysis, which they expect to occur during the fall and winter months:

(a) Northeast US customers tend to reduce their stock levels by 80% from October to March (b) Southeast sales have the potential to remain or even slightly grow during this same period; (c) shipping charges from Southeast Asia increase slightly; (d) energy costs for heating usually increase for the business' physical location.

The company came up with the following risk mitigation measures to offset the Northeast decrease in sales:

(a) Focus sales to customers from South Carolina to Florida; (b) conduct business trips to determine if an opportunity exists to increase distribution to Southeast customers and provide incentives for Northeast customers to increase their stocks for the spring surge (c) consult with Southeast Asian distributors to reduce orders but increase stocks of supplies later in the winter to be prepared for the spring (d) instead of hiring all permanent employees, hire seasonal employees to offset the lower output during the off-season.

Failure to identify trends during the development of the business plan may result in unnecessary changes or even over-corrections. Anticipating second- and third-order effects helps business owners prepare for potential and inevitable situations. Being prepared to take action and thinking through these situations is your way of having an insurance policy for situations that insurance companies don't cover. A good example of failure to identify trends may be:

BKCC failed to identify that the Northeast retailers reduce their stock six months out of the year. The second- and third-order effects are: (a) the company maintained its incoming stocks and ran out of storage space (b) the company maintained all full-time employees throughout the winter months despite not having sufficient work; (c) and the increased cost of shipping caused the company to continue to pay creditors for supplies that they couldn't sell.

Business owners who think through their course corrections are able to prevent "oversteering"—implementing excessive actions to fix a perceived problem. This action usually has a desired short-term effect of fixing the problem but negatively affects the situation for the long term. This is because oversteering creates shocks to the economic or physical system of the business (see Figure 3).

Generally speaking, shocks are bad and can force a business into colossal failure. Contrarily, it is possible but not likely that a shock can catapult a business into unexpected success. Unexpected successes can be considered the result of a social trend or popular cultural movement which sparks unanticipated purchases of a specific brand or type of material. Neither colossal failure nor unexpected success should be the foundation of a successful business plan. The aware entrepreneur understands the trends and implements the appropriate actions in order to maintain control over the business and forecast an upward trajectory despite recoverable setbacks.

Recoverable setbacks are either physical or financial situations that have trended south of being positive, but are within your expected zone of tolerance. With the application of the appropriate course correction and without expending excessive funding, physical or psychological energy, the business can move its trajectory back into trending positive.

As an analogy, let's say you are a business entrepreneur driving across the country. Before you start your journey, you should determine how much money and fuel you will consume. You may also want to know the best locations to rest and eat. You definitely would want to know which route to take, and you would need to decide how many hours you are able or want to drive in a day. In essence, you want to know where you are going, how you are going to get there, what part of the year to travel, why you are taking the trip and how you will accomplish it. This is your mission statement for the travel plan. But after you start your trip, you need to make sure that you are traveling along your planned route.

Since you have planned your route carefully, you are prepared for the execution of your trip. You developed waypoints to help you keep track of your progress. If you take a wrong turn, your planned benchmarks assist you in correcting your actions, preventing you from getting too far off course. As you conclude each day's travel, you pull out your map and determine if you are still on target. You conduct preventive maintenance by checking your fluids and checking the tires. You are prepared for environmental changes in case it rains or snows. When you approach an unexpected detour, you quickly determine your next actions.

This analogy should help the future entrepreneur to realize the importance of the analysis that leads to the development of the business plan. A plan that doesn't have benchmarks or measures of learning enables businesses to fail to conduct periodic assessments. Periodic assessments enable a business to determine if it is operating within its constraints and limitations and then make course corrections without oversteering.

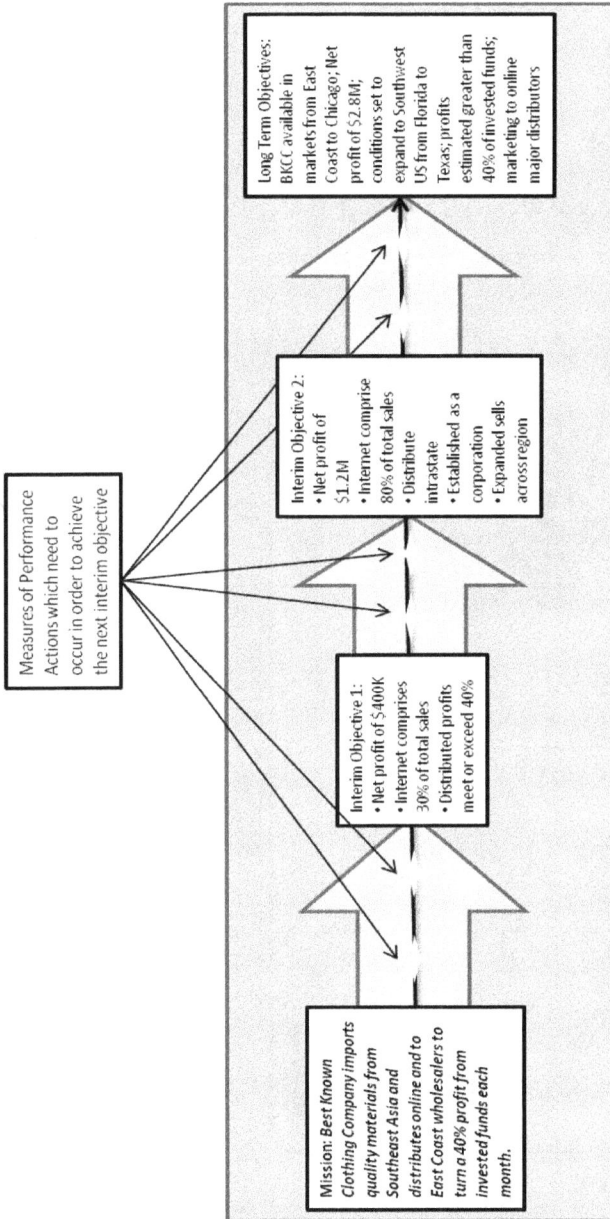

Measures of Performance
Actions which need to occur in order to achieve the next interim objective

Mission: Best Known Clothing Company imports quality materials from Southeast Asia and distributes online and to East Coast wholesalers to turn a 40% profit from invested funds each month.

Interim Objective 1:
• Net profit of $400K
• Internet comprises 30% of total sales
• Distributed profits meet or exceed 40%

Interim Objective 2:
• Net profit of $1.2M
• Internet comprise 80% of total sales
• Distribute intrastate
• Established as a corporation
• Expanded sells across region

Long Term Objectives:
BKCC available in markets from East Coast to Chicago; Net profit of $2.8M; conditions set to expand to Southwest US from Florida to Texas; profits estimated greater than 40% of invested funds; marketing to online major distributors

Figure 1

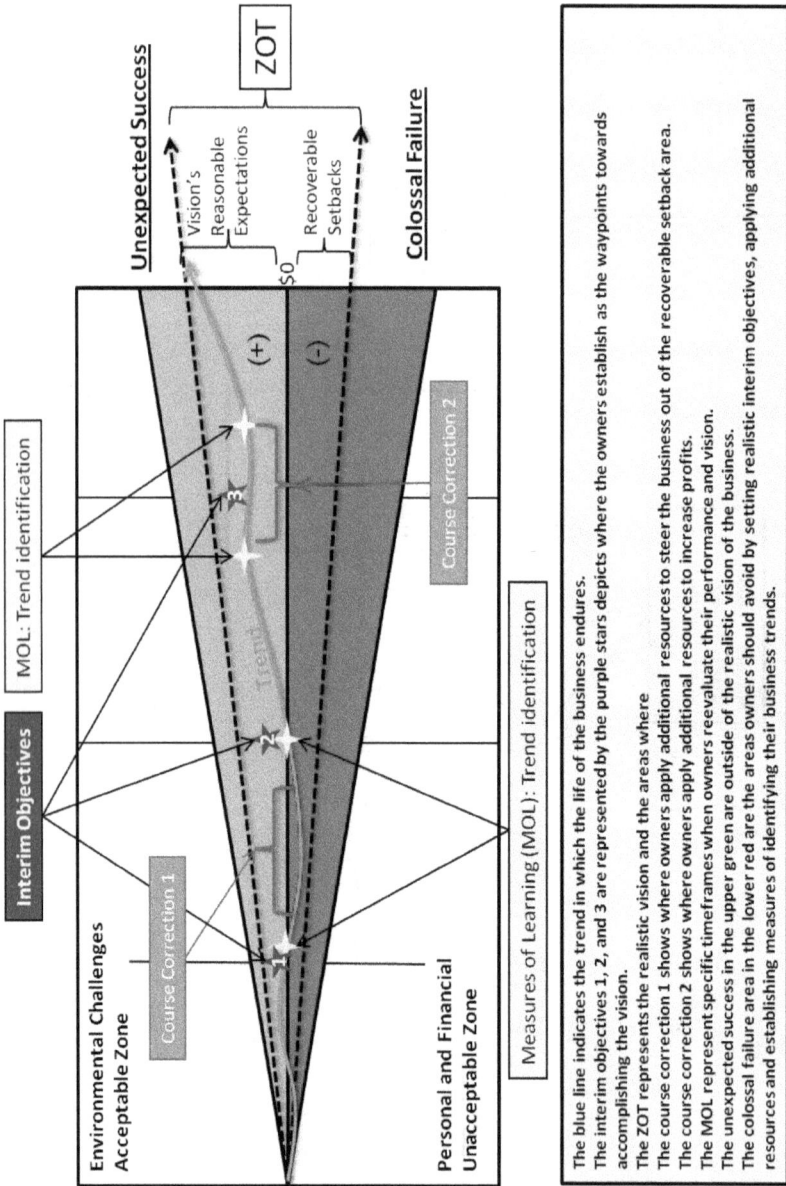

ZOT

Unexpected Success

Vision's
Reasonable
Expectations

Recoverable
Setbacks

Colossal Failure

$0

(+)

(−)

MOL: Trend identification

Interim Objectives

Environmental Challenges
Acceptable Zone

Course Correction 1

Course Correction 2

Trend

Personal and Financial
Unacceptable Zone

Measures of Learning (MOL): Trend identification

The blue line indicates the trend in which the life of the business endures.
The interim objectives 1, 2, and 3 are represented by the purple stars depicts where the owners establish as the waypoints towards accomplishing the vision.
The ZOT represents the realistic vision and the areas where
The course correction 1 shows where owners apply additional resources to steer the business out of the recoverable setback area.
The course correction 2 shows where owners apply additional resources to increase profits.
The MOL represent specific timeframes when owners reevaluate their performance and vision.
The unexpected success in the upper green are outside of the realistic vision of the business.
The colossal failure area in the lower red are the areas owners should avoid by setting realistic interim objectives, applying additional resources and establishing measures of identifying their business trends.

Figure 2

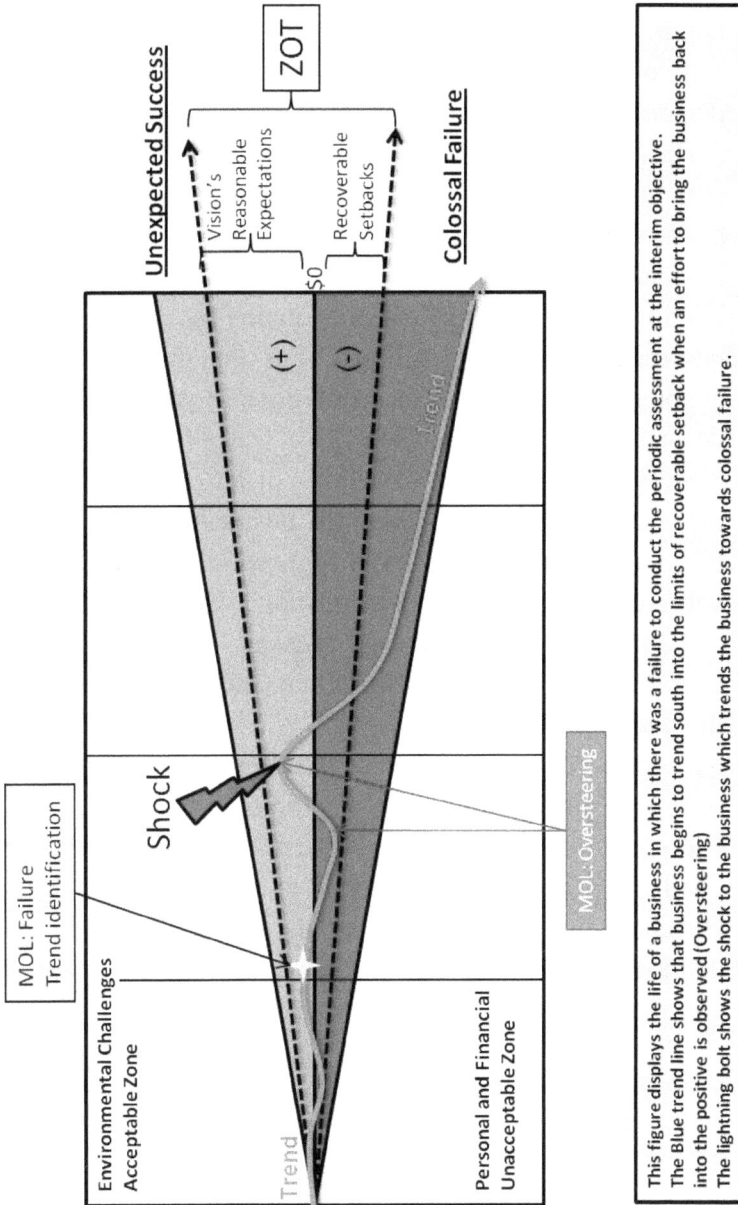

This figure displays the life of a business in which there was a failure to conduct the periodic assessment at the interim objective. The Blue trend line shows that business begins to trend south into the limits of recoverable setback when an effort to bring the business back into the positive is observed (Oversteering)
The lightning bolt shows the shock to the business which trends the business towards colossal failure.

Figure 3

Definitions

1. Constraint – According to Merriam-Webster's Online Dictionary (www.m-w.com), "constraint" is defined as the state of being checked, restricted, or compelled to avoid or perform some action. For this chapter, "constraint" is defined as the conditions necessary to maintain the structure of the business plan. Effectively, the real or psychological areas that a business should avoid entering.

2. Limitation – According to Merriam-Webster's Online Dictionary, "limitation" is the quality or state of being bound, restrained or confined. For the purposes of this chapter, "limitation" is the conditions in which the author defines the shape of the "box".

3. Vision – The long-term objective of an organization. It is the best interpretation of what the business can be.

4. Rational Action Theory – The suggestion that a person may want more than is actually achievable, when, in reality, one can only achieve what is within reason. Therefore one must conservatively expend energy, time, and/or finances to gain the maximum output.

5. Measures of Performance – Real and physical actions which reasonably lead to the desired effect.

6. Measures of Learning – Moments in time where one conducts a periodic assessment of where the business is currently and if the business is on trajectory towards achieving the long-term goals and nested with the entrepreneur's vision.

Suggested Reading

1. Naveh, Shimon, *In Pursuit of Military Excellence: The Evolution of Operational Theory.* London: Frank Cass, 1997.

2. United States Government: Department of the Army. *Army Field Manual FM 3-90: Tactics.* Washington, DC, 2001.

Kelly Marianno empowers through education and encouragement. He inspires through accountability; encouraging people to dig deeply within to reach goals and enjoy greater success.

I.M.P.A.K.T is a personal development organization he founded with his wife in June of 2009. It helps struggling entrepreneurs develop into focused business owners prepared to overcome goal reaching obstacles.

Mr. Marianno, a proud father of one daughter, has always been creatively ambitious. He began his rich and varied entrepreneurial quest at 18. The quest includes selling books through classified newspaper ads, selling and buying real estate, building a successful network marketing team and his most recent accomplishment; creating and leading I.M.P.A.K.T. His extensive study and experiences gained through developing entrepreneurs of all types give Mr. Marianno great insight into what small successful business owners need.

Contact Information:
www.makeimpakt.com
856-452-1551
kelly@makeimpakt.com

Chapter 8

Presenting Your Business to the World

Kelly Marianno

Congratulations! You are an entrepreneur! You have a great, unique idea, product or service that you believe in and want to offer to others. Whether you are full-time or part-time, you are an entrepreneur, striking out on our own. I applaud you as you step towards making your dreams come true. The applause is worthy not because of how long you have been in business, or how much money you have made. Applause is merited even if you have yet to serve your first client. It is merited because you have the courage to endure unforeseen challenges and bring your dreams to life. So give yourself a hand. As you follow the critical steps in this chapter, you will be empowered to present to the world and most importantly, to your potential clients, a professional image.

Your potential clients are bombarded with advertisements and marketing tactics designed to make their choice of who to do business with easier. Do not make it easy for them to eliminate your business as a viable option because you have decided to take a shortcut. Shortcuts include handing them a homemade business card (unless it represents a unique characteristic of your business) or subjecting them to a dated website on your product or service. More on these later, but suffice to say, that your clients may likely be looking for what you offer, just don't give them a reason to go elsewhere when you can represent yourself and your brand well, even if you are on a budget. This chapter will provide direction on how to implement a professional image and meet the unspoken expectations of your clients.

If your business endeavor involves a network marketing venture or a franchise, some of the points discussed in this chapter will not immediately apply to you. This is because some of the areas addressed in this guide will be done for you by the corporation that you represent. However, keep reading, there will definitely be something that you can apply or simply share with others.

I, like you, am an entrepreneur. I have spent years helping other entrepreneurs in one aspect of their businesses or another. My name is Kelly Marianno, founder of IMPAKT, a personal development company designed to help entrepreneurs become more profitable in their respective businesses. Among the many things we do, we offer coaching, motivational talks, tools and services in support of increasing the entrepreneur's profits.

While many folks aspire to help make others more profitable through various means whether they are called plans or secrets, this chapter is devoted to a more practical approach to the do's and don'ts of setting up, running, and the monetizing of your business endeavor. This practical approach will include some simple step by step guidelines that you can transfer directly from this book to your to-do list. This minimizes the excuses we often hide behind when failure arrives at our door. While I am on the subject of failure, I do not believe that failure is something to be avoided but is merely a milestone of sorts on one's way to ultimate success. That being said, this guide is for you if you want to get off to a good start as an entrepreneur.

This guide will address three major areas for an entrepreneur to consider. The first area is the first impression phase. This is how you choose to present your business to the world before any business is transacted. The second phase is the engagement process. During this part, some level of engagement has generally been initiated and the client/customer is at least in the consideration phase of doing business with you. The last phase is the lasting impression phase. This is where you leave the client not only willing to recommend you, but perhaps even seeking opportunities to encourage others to do business with you. This last section is often overlooked by many entrepreneurs but from now on, it will be given the attention that it deserves. It has been said that one only gets one chance at a first impression. Make it memorable.

Well, making a moment memorable isn't really a specific enough goal. It needs to be memorable in a positive fashion. You want to make sure that you stand out from the crowd in a way that makes your business the first to come to mind when your client is ready to do business with a company such as yours. Some of the things that will be discussed may not have any impact on your ability to do business effectively but if you are going to do business it is worth doing it the right way. Follow the steps in this guide to get your business setup correctly from the beginning.

I am going to continue with an assumption that you have made a decision on a product or service to represent or make available to potential clients and customers. In order to make this guide as useful as possible, I will place many of these steps in a bulleted list so that you can take each section and copy each item into to your to-do list. As laws vary from state to state, I won't get too far into the legal requirements, but I will share with you what was necessary in my case if I think it is relevant. With that being said, it is time to list the first area we will address: your business name.

Tips for creating a business name:

- Avoid names that could be offensive to your potential client
- Avoid names that may alienate your clients (i.e. slang terms or cultural terms that would imply that you only want customers from a particular culture.)
- Consider a name that clearly indicates what your business offers as a product or service.
- Choose a name, when possible, that is catchy and perhaps easy to remember. (not appropriate for all businesses)
- Make sure the name you come up with isn't already being used on the county, state or federal level depending on the type of business structure you choose. Also, avoid names that are too similar to another. You could inherit a bad reputation. (*Don't get any promotional items printed until this has been resolved)
- Create a business name that reflects the image of your business that you want to present to clients. Kelly Marianno's Company is very different from Marianno Enterprises, Inc. *Don't use "Inc. or LLC" after your business name unless you have established your company as that business type.
- Be creative, original or even provocative with your name. Don't just pick something because it is easy or cheaper to establish.

Once you have identified a business name, it will be important to make that name your own through legal ownership. However, before you do that it will be equally important for you to choose a business entity. The reason for this is that your business type may be reflected in the business name and determines how and with whom the name is filed. Determining what type of business you want to establish is beyond the scope of this chapter but I will say that I would encourage you to not just pick what others have done because it is a popular choice. I have mentioned this already but I would also warn against doing a particular business choice like sole proprietorship because of how easy it is to establish or the low cost involved. Speak with someone who understands the formation of these types of entities and who understands the tax implications. A friend of mine chose the wrong one (through the advice of a CPA) and it cost him $10,000 per year in additional taxes. Don't make a mistake like that because you didn't want to do your due diligence. He did his due diligence, which is how the problem was identified but the money was already lost. Once you have that business name and type, you need to consider the next steps.

Tips for what to do after the name and business type has been determined:

- File the necessary forms to establish your business as the entity that you have determined is right for you.
- If you believe a website is in the future of your company, secure your URL (web address) today. This will prevent others from obtaining your name. Below are the steps to take.
  - Go to a site that hosts websites or sells domains such as GoDaddy.com.
  - Search for your name. (For example, if your company is named My Company you might search for www.mycompany.com, or for a non-profit, you might choose www.mynonprofit.org. The ".org" implies not profit or similar entity.)

- o Once you obtain an available URL, register it. Even if you don't use it now, it is well worth the small investment to hold the name.
- Consider purchasing additional URL's if you believe it may be advantageous for your business. (For example, I am developing myself as a motivational or empowerment speaker so I purchased www.KellyMarianno.com for this endeavor even though I am not sure when I will use it.)

Consider whether or not you should also purchase the other domains such as .org or .net when purchasing your URL. Doing so does not mean that your website needs to be built numerous times. Nor does it entail paying additional URL hosting fees. Simply have your website developer forward the additional URLs to your main site. For example, you now own www.mynonprofit.org but you want to make sure that if your site visitor types in www.mynonprofit.com by mistake, they will get forwarded to the correct URL, which in this case is www.mynonprofit.org. This can only happen if you also purchased www.mynonprofit.com and you or your developer has forwarded the .com entry to the official .org website. Without these two steps (purchasing of the additional URL and the forwarding), the client would receive an error message because there is no website at that location.

You now have your company name, business type and websites or at least the information necessary to establish them. The next step is your promotional material. Promotional material covers many things including business cards, flyers, websites (the copy or wording on them), brochures and practically any other material used for generating revenue. Promotional materials are an extension of your business and provide a first impression. This is not an area for producing cheap materials. Use quality products or at least, the best quality you can afford. In some cases, it may be advantageous to go without certain materials if quality products cannot be produced at an affordable price. Using less than high quality gives clients a mixed message. You want them to take you and your business seriously, so be consistent and do not give clients promotional materials that suggest otherwise. A perfect example of this is the perforated business cards. They suggest I am in business but not doing well enough to afford $50.00-$100.00 for good business cards. Do not send this message.

Tips regarding your promotional materials:

- Avoid perforated and printed at home business cards especially those on light weight card stock.
- Business cards should have the appropriate contact information.
- Business cards should indicate what you or your business does so that the client knows why he should contact you. Don't assume that your client knows what you do because you told him or her.
- Avoid non-professional email addresses on your business cards such as Yahoo, AOL, Gmail and other free email. When possible, use an email address that ties into your business such as johndoe@mycompany.com. It shows cohesiveness and implies permanence.
- Don't hand out materials with stains on it. (Especially as a caterer.)

- Don't distribute materials with information crossed out or handwritten. If something has changed or is missing, look at the need to reproduce the materials as the cost of doing business.
- Make sure that your website has the look and feel of a conventional website.
- Make sure that your website functions well and in a manner that is consistent with what consumers expect today. Have someone else test it and get feedback.
- Make sure that your website has...
  - a contact page to request information
  - a form to subscribe to your site or email campaign
  - effective copy that has a call to action
  - an effective means to transact business directly from the site, if applicable.
- Use quality photos or professional photos from a stock photo site.

Keep in mind that you only get one chance to make a first impression. Don't blow it because you think that it is not that important, or that others won't notice or will understand that you are a new entrepreneur. It is possible that others will not notice but what if they do? Don't risk pointing potential clients towards your competitors because you have decided to take a shortcut. And if clients can be swayed away, it is that important! We have discussed making a good impression and its importance, but once you have engaged the client, you will want to do business in a professional manner as well.

One way for you to help yourself to be and remain professional is to treat people the way that you want to be treated. If you are about to do something for a client and have a thought that it is "good enough" or "that will do," then you are probably getting ready to short change your client in some way. Don't do it! Rethink it! Reproduce it if necessary but don't let anything leave your hands (or your business) that does not reflect pride. A good rule of thumb is giving more value than they are requesting and not just enough. Keep in mind that no matter what product or service you are promoting, you are in the customer service industry. You are constantly thinking of serving your customer first. We must have the right attitude while serving clients. Below are tips that encourage clients to do and continue to do business with you.

Tips to providing excellent customer service to your clients:
- Deliver products and services on time as promised (I had a boss once that said, "Under promise and over deliver.")
  - If you have been delivering your products/services in a tardy fashion, correct it by finding efficiencies in your process to shorten time to delivery or by setting an expectation for a longer delivery window so that you can be on time for your clients.
  - If it takes you 7 to 10 days to produce something, don't give the clients a 7 to 10 day window for delivery. Advise them that it will take two weeks for delivery so when it comes early, you will be seen as having great service.
  - Notify clients of delays in delivery as soon as the possibility becomes evident.
- Treat clients with respect and honor
- Accept checks in the name of your business

- o Once you have your business name registered, you can take the registration information to the bank in order to establish this ability.
- Accept credit cards. (It is no longer difficult to get the ability to accept credit cards)
  - o Look online for "accepting credit cards" or specific vendors such as PayPal, Intuit or "the Square".

While some of these things are common sense, they are worth mentioning so that they are kept in mind. The checks and credit card components are two that may not seem as obvious, but not accepting credit cards can present an inconvenience in today's world where credit/debit cards are used more than cash. Not being able to accept a check in your business name implies that you aren't seriously in business. This is also implied if your business has one name but the client has to address the check to an individual. These tips are simple in implementation, but make a big difference in perception. Client perception leads us to the next section; leaving an impression that compels clients to tell their friends and families about us.

At this point, we have made a good impression. We have done business well. Now, the question is, "What steps do we take to ensure that the experience has been memorable and therefore our clients will want to provide referrals?" Before sharing these tips, I caution you to avoid the mistake of thinking that clients will remember you because you are friends or even family. Give them a reason to think about you. Give them an incentive to refer you to others.

Tips to have your clients send you referrals:
- Request feedback from clients, when appropriate, to uncover possible discontent.

- Address areas of low customer satisfaction quickly. (Bad experiences get shared quickly. Don't have a bad experienced "tweeted" if it is possible to have addressed it before it gets to that point.)
- Develop a newsletter or on-going correspondence that is NOT simply a sales brochure and is distributed at least quarterly.
- If your product or service is needed on-going, follow up with the client to remind him when it is time to purchase again.
- Develop a referral incentive program that reward clients for sending purchasing clients to you.
- Give more value than the client expects

These are just some ways to encourage clients to refer you to others. Pay attention to what your competitors are doing and use new ideas that you feel will work with your clientele. You will rarely be disappointed with referral clients because much of the trust and rapport is already established by virtue of the referral. Don't take that for granted. Use it to develop a quicker deeper bond with new clients.

In this chapter we have discussed things that entrepreneurs need to consider when establishing a business, doing business and when nurturing an on-going client/entrepreneur relationship. You can ignore everything in this chapter and have a good business. However, if you want a great business, implement these tips today. Your rewards will be felt in your bottom line. You will have the pleasure of knowing that you did the best job that you could do for your clients.

Maggie Steele is a life coach for teens and young adults and the author of *How I Got My S!*t Together: An Introspective Workbook to Help You Find Your Passion and Purpose In Life*. She has coached both adolescents and adults on her journey and is passionate about giving her clients the tools they need to recognize and overcome self-limiting beliefs. She believes that every single person, no matter what their past experiences may be, is capable of realizing their dreams, being successful, and finding fulfillment in their life. As a certified life coach and career coach, Maggie helps young people from all different backgrounds recognize their strengths and pinpoint their passion. Her coaching methods have given many young people the confidence to pursue their dreams, overcome challenges, stop unwanted behavior and become the person they want to be. Maggie is also an entertaining youth speaker and host of *Younique Tv,* a web series in which she gives advice to teens and young adults. She contributes inspirational articles to various magazines across the United States and can be contacted for coaching sessions, workshops and assemblies.

Learn more at:

www.TheLifeCoachForTeens.com

Chapter 9

Overcoming Rejection

Maggie Steele

While many of us are more than happy to share our personal achievements and feel quite comfortable discussing ambitious goals, our eagerness often wanes when it comes to revealing the rejections and past failures we have experienced. More often than not, we keep our stories of rejection to ourselves, assuming others will judge us or think differently of our accomplishments if we disclose the numerous times we were, in fact, told that our work just didn't cut it. What many of us seem to forget is that all of us have at one time or another, been flat out refused, and that even those who have reached the oh-so-sought-after-summit-of-success, had to overcome countless rejections and heartbreaking failures on the way.

Stephen King may be a celebrity author today, but years ago the unknown writer started out with a big dream and a book he called *Carrie*. King's dream was swiftly crushed when *Carrie* was promptly rejected by thirty different publishers. If King had stopped there, would he have become the bestselling author he is today and would *Carrie* have become the cult thriller it eventually became?

Probably not. Sidney Poitier, one of America's most respected actors, was told at one of his very first auditions to throw in the towel and become a dishwasher instead. Imagine if he had! Poitier, however, pushed on with his dream and ended up with an Oscar and a great deal of admiration from those in the entertainment industry.

Walt Disney's dream to build a magical theme park was crushed numerous times and he ended up going bankrupt three times before his dream came true. While there are countless stories of perseverance and courage, one of my favorites belongs to Kathryn Stockett, author of *The Help.* Stockett was rejected 60 times from various publishers and was told by her family and friends to write something else. Stockett stuck to her guns and went on to be a best-selling author with a major film deal that garnered four academy award nominations including best picture.

If you take a moment now to look back on your life, I am certain that you will recall some of your own glorious setbacks. Your eyes, while blurry with salty frustration back then, are likely to see quite clearly today all of the brilliant things born out of that very same devastation. Perhaps that dream job that passed you by gave you the courage to pursue a different path, or that promotion you never received strengthened your resolve and helped you decide to go back to school. Think about your own personal heartbreaks and see what good came of those dismal days. Just how many doors swung open in different areas of your life when others slammed in your face? As painful as it may be, rejection, it seems, is a vital stepping stone on our path to success. If we try to side step these potential let downs or even worse, avoid them entirely, we will make little progress and end up in a perpetual state of tolerability. If you have read this far, I highly doubt that you are someone who is interested in settling! So here is the hard truth: If you want to be successful, you have to take risks. Now please don't misunderstand me. I'm not talking about jumping head first into a business endeavor without having done the appropriate research or made the necessary preparations. Taking risks should not be confused with acting carelessly. Instead, taking a risk means taking a bold and courageous step toward the future you envision.

Choosing to step out of your comfort zone is, in itself, an audacious act that takes a great deal of nerve and tenacity. And while the benefits that await you are far greater than those in your old state of tolerability, stepping outside of the world you've come to know is not always a pleasant experience. Venturing into new territory can prove to be frightening and the little voice inside your head will make sure that its reservations are heard. Doubts and fears will surface, pushing you to question the very risk you took. Suddenly failure will become a real possibility forcing you to throw in the towel and turn around, leaving behind a trail of excuses and forgotten dreams.

Sadly, this is what many of us do. We take that bold step toward our dreams and soon after walk away, overcome with the notion of failure and impossibility. So this is where you have to ask yourself a very important question. Would you rather live a life in which everything is tolerable, or do you want to take advantage of this unknown amount of time and live the dream life you envision? Think about that. Seriously consider what you want and what it means to you to realize your dreams. Once you are certain that you are done with settling, you can start focusing on what steps need to be taken on your path to fulfillment, and how you are going to face the rejection, failure, and heartache that will most certainly accompany you on your way. In order to face these difficult moments, we must first recognize what happens to us when we are rejected. Most of us end up taking rejection personally and see it not just as a reflection of our work, but as a way of assessing our value as a person. After all, we are sharing a part of ourselves with someone who ultimately gets to decide whether or not we are, in fact, worthy. We have, in effect, chosen to hand over our self worth, our personal power, and allow someone else to determine whether or not we are good enough. It should come as no surprise then, that feelings of hurt, anger, sadness, and frustration should surface when we are suddenly told by this person that we are, in a sense, worthless.

You are, of course, not worthless and there are various things you can do to overcome the emotional hurt these rejections and refusals may cause.

> *Emotions often triggered by refusals stem from past experiences, and are not typically linked to the situation at hand.*

Childhood is riddled with moments that stay with us, etched in our hearts and heads, motivating our behavior and directing our actions. While you may not remember the first time you were told that you were not good enough, the feeling nevertheless remains. Just as a scab will not heal if scratched, the hurt that once was will resurface if provoked. It is for this reason that rejection can be so painful and so personal. Each "No" seems like a validation of sorts, telling us that our feelings are justified and that we are, in fact, not good enough.

Once you understand why rejection is so painful and powerful enough to keep you from realizing your dreams, you can then focus your energy on how to overcome it. While it is clear that you will likely face rejections on your path to success, there is no reason for you to waste time wallowing in the anguish it often leaves behind. There are several ways to push forward and below you will find four steps to help you combat the emotional blockage that refusals frequently instigate.

1. Identify the Exact Emotions

Often times we become so entrenched in our emotions, that we are unable to let them go. One of the keys to overcoming rejection is to identify the specific feelings evoked when you have been refused. Ask yourself, what do I feel when someone tells me they are not interested? Am I surprised by their disinterest? Do I feel slightly hurt, or is it a deep heartache at having been tossed to the side? Once you are able to pinpoint the exact emotions you are experiencing, write them down and step away. Give yourself some time and come back to the words you have written. Look at the specific adjectives you used to describe your frustration and pain. Recognize that the pain you are feeling is a reflection of a past hurt, feel it fully and let it go.

2. Reconnect With Your Dream

Another effective method to combat the emotional response that often accompanies rejection is by taking a rest and refocusing. Belief in yourself and in your dream is imperative if you want to succeed. By reconnecting with your dream you can accept the rejection as a minor setback and continue on. Take a moment to yourself and visualize the future you desire.

Ask yourself a few key questions. What is your typical day like in this future life? What is your work environment like? How does your future self feel about past challenges now? When you ask yourself these questions be sure to get specific. The more detail, the more real it becomes and the more real it is, the easier it is to believe. Once you believe that this future life is possible, you can let go of your current setback and recognize it for what it is; a minor bump in the road on your path to success.

3. Create a Powerful Mantra

Giving yourself a personal mantra that helps you refocus can be a very productive way to move forward as well. Think about what your mission means to you, strengthen your resolve, and make sure that no amount of doubt will ever stop you from realizing your dream. Come up with an inspirational sentence that amps you up, keeps you determined, and helps you move forward. Put it where you can see it every morning and continue on your mission. If rejection rears its ugly head again (and in all honesty, I can promise that it will) take a few breaths, repeat your mantra, and let its truth resonate and carry on.

4. Get Rid of Any Doubt

Rejection is often followed by thoughts of doubt and confusion. Suddenly we feel uncertain as to whether or not our dream is possible. Deep rooted fears take over and stand in our way, forcing us to second guess all that we had so strongly believed in before. When these doubts appear, our mission becomes impossible and our dream a highly unlikely, unrealistic endeavor. You have two choices at this point. You can either stop your mission, turn around and walk back into the land of tolerability, or you can reassess, refocus and reestablish the momentum you will need to get back on track.

Ask yourself the following questions the next time you are confronted with doubt and see what happens.

6 Questions To Ask Yourself When Confronted With Doubt After Rejection
1. What exactly am I feeling?
2. What can I do right now that will help me let go and push forward?
3. Do I feel pressure to give up my dream?
4. Am I willing to give up my dream?
5. What is it that I ultimately want?
6. What can I learn from this?

It is unfortunate that so many of us try to navigate the road of life by keeping our distance and staying far away from the potential hazards that we fear will slow us down or keep us from getting to our final destination. What we fail to understand, however, is that the very obstacles we are so desperately trying to avoid, are actually valuable opportunities disguised as adversity. Learn to surmount the challenges you are confronted with and embrace the rejections that come your way, for in the end, they are not there to hinder you, but to help you and propel you to greater heights.

> *Success, when all is said and done, is nothing but the result of having tried and failed over and over again.*

Mike lives and breathes marketing. Born and raised in Phoenix, Arizona, he has achieved most of his business success on the Internet. Mike has taught Marketing Positioning Techniques to thousands around the globe. Mike lives his life purpose of teaching and helping people grow personally and professionally, with a passion/mission of *"leaving this world a better place than I found it."* He is a Certified Marketer, speaker, teacher, copywriter, web site developer, business consultant and entrepreneur who enjoys getting business owners to their next level by crafting the right message for the right audience.

Mike loves studying human psychology, understanding why people do what they do, and applying this understanding to marketing business models. He enjoys studying how to get people to buy. Mike also has a deeply spiritual core and lives a life of peace and integrity. In 2010, he adopted a plant-based diet and various alternative healing therapies out of a desire to elevate his health to new levels.

Mike is a life-long learner with two Bachelor's degrees, one in Business Administration and one in Marketing, from the University of Phoenix and an M.B.A. in Management from Western International University. He says, *"The day I stop learning will be the day I die."* He is a member of Delta Mu Delta and Golden Key International Honor Societies. He is also an avid student of Western Tropical Astrology.

Contact information:
mike.lewitz@gmail.com
www.mikelewitz.com
(602) 445-6305

Chapter 10

Solving Your Customer's Problems
Mike Lewitz

"If you can describe a person's problem better than they can, they will automatically and unconsciously credit you with knowing the answer."
Wyatt Woodsmall

The fundamental purpose of any business is to solve a person's problem. If your business doesn't solve someone's problem, then you don't have a business.

The term *problem* is used loosely here. For example, someone's problem might be: I want to be entertained. A movie theater is an option that solves their problem. The way to solve your customer's problem is to create value for them.

What exactly is "value," and how do you determine what value is to your customer?

Value is whatever your customer says it is. Determining what value is to your customer is your challenge.

Unfortunately, your future customers are not going to tell you what value is to them. They are not going to come up to you one day and say, "Here's what we would find valuable and if you do/make this for us, we'll come to you and buy it." It is up to you to figure it out. This chapter gives you the step-by-step of how to figure out exactly what your customer finds valuable.

Determining what value is to your customer requires you to get to know your customer. You need to get inside his or her head. When you truly understand the needs of your customer and the problems they want solved, you can then create solutions that directly address those needs and problems with solutions they find valuable, and your products and services will essentially sell themselves.

Your Frame Of Reference

Always ask, "What is my customer thinking and experiencing?"
Your next customer does not know you, like you, or trust you. As far as they are concerned, you are just another crook trying to take their money, promising the best widget and amazing customer service...just like every other dishonest businessperson out there. Your customer does not care about you and will never be as interested as you are in what you have to offer.

The ONLY thing your customer cares about is what they're going to get.

So, it does not matter what you think is important and valuable. What only matters is what your customer thinks value is. Your product or service, the packaging, and even the words you use all must come from your customer's perspective of their problem and what he or she believes will improve their situation. Everything should only be about them.

If you want to make real money and become financially wealthy and have a business that pays you while you sleep, you need to know *precisely* what your customer thinks is important, from their *emotional* viewpoint, and not from a logical, rational viewpoint (more on this in a bit).

I harp on the importance of understanding your customer's emotional viewpoint a lot because its effective application is critical to the success of your business. Sadly, few ever consider their customer's emotional viewpoint. This is the crux of most business successes...and failures. Most business owners act on what their intuition drives them to do, only concerned with what they want to give their customers. Unfortunately, they are looking through the wrong end of the telescope.

Michael Gerber, author of *The E-Myth*, says, "More than 80 percent of all businesses fail within the first five years." Of the remaining 20 percent, Gerber states, "More than 80 percent of the small businesses that survive the first five years fail in the second five."[1] That's a 96 percent failure rate in business within 10 years. In other words, there is a 96 percent chance your business will fail within 10 years. The odds are heavily stacked against you.

Still, some businesses succeed far beyond any expectation. What's the difference? Ask people who have had a business that failed, "What would've made the difference?" Most will likely say, "I didn't have enough customers. If I had more customers, my business would have survived."

While the real solution is complex, the vast majority of business owners are operating only on their intuition and rarely (if ever) consider their customer's perspective, because they believe they know their customers better than they actually do.

Decades ago, it was okay to be sloppy in business. Consumers had significantly fewer choices, most products were domestic, communication was often delayed (or lost), and there was no Internet. Today, oceans and international borders mean nothing in business. Communication is automated and instantaneous. Your mouse movements and browsing time are tracked to the microsecond to see how long you spend reading a web page before you leave or buy. Untold volumes of data are available from several data-gathering companies to any of your competitors willing to pay the asking price. If you are slightly off your game, your competition will quickly step in.

You must NEVER assume you completely understand your customer and that your message resonates with them. Get to know your customer through relentless, personalized research, surveys, and data-gathering to figure out what has the most influence on their buying decisions. Today, you can do this easily and inexpensively, and, in many cases, for free.

The bottom line is this: If you don't really *get* your customers and understand their perspective and what's important to them on a deep, internal level, you are going to have some really difficult challenges in business; you won't get the results you want and you will have no power and influence.

On the other hand, if you really understand what is important to your customer on a deep, emotional level, you will be able to create far better products and services and they will practically sell themselves. As well, you will influence more people, you will attract the types of people you want, both as customers and business partners, you will be able to achieve the goals you want, and you will have more power overall in your life.

Eben Pagan, a highly successful, self-made business man, says, "Success in business is not obvious and often counter-intuitive." Delivering value is no exception to Eben Pagan's statement.

Always ask, "What is my customer thinking and experiencing?"

Humans Are Irrational

To solve your customer's problem and create value for them, you must first get inside their mind and figure out what motivates them to buy so you can give them what they want, because the only thing that matters in your business is whether or not your next customer finds you and then buys from you.

So, how do you do this?

First, it is important you understand and recognize that we humans are completely irrational. We want to believe we are logical and rational. We even have a mechanism in our brain that convinces us we are, but we are not. This is difficult for most people to accept and wrap their brain around, but the sooner you are able to understand and accept it, the more quickly you will get results.

Over the past few years, modern technology has given us tremendously powerful insight into how the human brain works. You can directly apply this information to get inside the mind of your customers and make more money by solving their problems better.

A popular model of how the human brain works is called the *triune* brain. This model says we actually have three brains stacked on top of each other instead of just one: a reptilian 'old' brain that sits on top of the brain stem and controls physical survival and maintenance functions like breathing and digestion, a mammalian 'middle' brain (sometimes called the *chimpanzee* brain) that controls emotions and smell, and the neocortex 'new' brain that controls things like logic, language and planning.

As human beings, each one of us is driven by our passions, feelings and emotions ...and so are your customers.

There is a ton of evidence on this, so I'm not going to get into how we know. For now, you're just going to have to take my word for it. If you always come from the point of view that humans function completely on and are driven entirely by their chimpanzee 'emotional' brain, you will get far better results and make a lot more money. Only emotions create action, and thoughts create emotions, which also create more thoughts. Therefore, the ONLY way to get *any* action from your customer is you must trigger an emotion.

THOUGHTS → EMOTIONS → ACTION

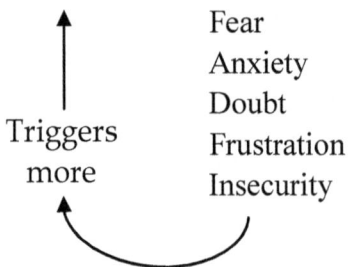

Fear

Anxiety

Doubt

Triggers more

Frustration

Insecurity

Eugene Schwartz, a highly successful copywriter and the author of *Breakthrough Advertising*, says when you're communicating with your prospects, you're not talking to the logical brain, you're talking to the *chimpanzee* brain. The *emotional* brain.

So, to figure out your customer's problem, start by asking, "What is my customer's emotional experience (in relationship to my product or service)?" You need to know what's going on inside the *chimpanzee* brain, not the logical brain.

If you can grasp just this one idea of understanding what's going on inside your customer's chimpanzee brain and then apply it to trigger a buying action, you will be miles ahead of your competition and even steal their customers away from them, because most business owners will *never* reach this level.

It's Never About Your Product
There's a saying, "People buy solutions, not products." People do not want a drill…they want a hole. People don't want your product or service. They want the benefit and outcome it provides. Actually, they want the *feeling* the outcome provides. On some subconscious level, your customers view your product or service as an obstacle that stands between them and the outcome they want to get because they cannot have the outcome and the feeling they want until they get your product or buy your service. They do not want laundry detergent, they want the feeling of looking and smelling good in clean clothes …or they want to avoid the bad feeling that comes from wearing clothes that are dirty and smelly, and to get that feeling, they have to spend money on your thing or buy your service.

If you act like you've got some miracle, people will disconnect from you and avoid you. However, if you view your product or service as if it is an obstacle to them, it will be easier for you to present it to them because you'll be coming from their perspective.

Getting inside your customer's head is a three-step process: create a *customer avatar*, describe their *emotional state*, and then determine their *hot buttons*.

STEP 1: Create Your Customer Avatar

"Bad business ideas almost always come down to not thinking like a customer. There is magical power in feeling understood. Compassion is the key, and possibly the ultimate money-making skill."
Eben Pagan

To think like your customers and identify with them on a deep, intimate level, it is very important you understand their situation, their routine, and their day-to-day life and experiences. If you fail to deeply understand your customer's perspective, your communication will be limited, you won't connect well, and you'll have difficulty building trust.

People who don't trust you will never buy from you.

The absolute best way to understand your customer, and the method used by the most successful marketers, is to write out a biography of your ideal customer, called a 'customer avatar.'

Your 'customer avatar' is a biographical outline of the person who is most likely to buy from you. It is the person who is out there actively looking for what you've got to offer and believes they *must* have your product the moment they discover it.

Get a sheet of paper and write out a description of this person. Imagine they are sitting directly across from you. Maybe you even have an actual customer in mind who has bought from you in the past. Get inside his or her head and pull out everything that relates to their needs, wants, and desires. You want to know what their day-to-day routine is like. Describe them in as much detail as possible. Make it long. Write as much as you can.

- Are they male or female?
- How old are they?
- What do they do for a living?
- Are they married?
- Do they have a girlfriend or boyfriend?
- Do they have any kids? How many?
- What do they like to do for fun?
- What kind of a place do they live in?
- What is the neighborhood like?
- Give him or her a name.
- Consider other information that is relevant to your specific product or service.

You cannot guess or assume *any* of these list items. Most business owners just guess, and, remember, most businesses fail. If you're not absolutely <u>certain</u> of these elements, you must do some research. Most business owners just want to jump right in and do what they think will best solve their customer's problem, but this is a HUGE mistake. Highly successful companies spend weeks, often months on just research...and there's a reason why. The extra time it takes to gather this priceless information will mean the difference between struggling to get customers and struggling to find enough employees to take orders.

Communicate with your existing customers. Get personal. Call them on the phone. Use social media to directly interact with them. Create a poll or survey. Web sites like surveymonkey.com and freeonlinesurveys.com will help you easily gather and analyze valuable data, often for free.

If you are just starting out and have no customers yet, conducting research upfront is an absolute must. I cannot tell you how many struggling clients I have worked with that were certain of their customer avatar, only to discover they were completely wrong after doing some simple research. Don't make this foolish, short-sighted mistake, or it will create a lot of expensive frustrations for you. Research is *not* optional.

STEP 2: Describe Their Emotional State
Solving your customer's problem involves communicating with them concisely in their language, using the emotional words and imagery that resonate with them, not what resonates with you. When you communicate with your customer using the exact same words that are inside his or her head, he or she connects with you and feels you understand them better than anyone else does. It feels magical to them.

After you've written your customer avatar and given him or her a name, start focusing on the emotional aspects of his or her life. Begin to think about and write down the details of what is happening in their life and how it's going.

Imagine how this person *feels* about the area of his or her life your product or service helps improve and the problems it solves.
- What are their frustrations?
- What do they struggle with?
- What are the good things (hopes, desires, aspirations)?

- What are the bad things?
- What are they unhappy about?

For example, if you sell a weight loss product, describe how your 'avatar' person feels about his or her body weight. How overweight are they - 10lbs or 150lbs? Be exact. Imagine all the different frustrations they have with being overweight, such as rude people, having to buy clothing from a special store, uncomfortable airline seats, and being called names. Maybe they dream about going to their high school reunion thin and muscular. Maybe they hate the 'fat' person they see in the mirror.

If you have a conversation with someone who is unhappy about some aspect of their life, it will not take long to figure out the person or thing outside of them they are blaming for their unhappiness. The reason why you can do this is because a person can only have the emotion of unhappiness as long as they blame it on someone or something outside of them. In other words, a person can only be unhappy if they blame it on someone or something else. They are creating a *fantasy* in their head.

- *"If my boss would have given me that raise, then I would be happy."*
- *"If that girl would have given me her phone number, I would feel better."*
- *"If my husband wasn't such a jerk, I would be happy in my marriage."*

Remember, emotions are what drive your customers to take action, and emotions happen in the *chimpanzee* brain, not the logical brain.

It is extremely important to grasp the previous concept because, since your customers believe their problem is caused by something outside of them, they believe their solution will be found outside of them, so that is where they are going to look. This is when they will discover your product or service.

So, when you are imagining and describing their emotional state, look for unmet emotional needs linked to externally rationalized causes.

Example: *"I'm overweight because my wife doesn't cook healthy food."* Ask yourself, "What is the *irrational fear* or *fantasy* going on inside their head?"

Write out their emotional state in graphic detail. Use words that are emotional and expressive.

Again, if you are not 100 percent certain of their emotional state, you must use research to find out. In a conversation or survey you could ask, "What's your greatest fear around situation X?" Be sure to make note of the exact, specific words they give you. These are the words inside their head.

STEP 3: Determine Their Hot Buttons

There are only two basic reasons why people do things: either to get something they want or to avoid some kind of pain or loss. Most purchases are driven more by negative emotions than positive ones. In either case, somewhere there is an unmet emotional need driving them to take some kind of action that will result in a purchasing decision, whether it's driven by a negative emotion or the lack of a positive one. For example, people are emotionally driven to buy body deodorant because either they want to smell nice, or they want to avoid the pain of embarrassment from having bad body odor. You create value for your customer by figuring out what they want to <u>get</u> and what they want to <u>avoid</u>.

So, in relationship to the outcome your product or service offers, you need to ask, What is their unmet emotional need? What does he or she want to change, and why? Why do they want to get this area of their life handled? What are his or her fears around this area of their life?

Go deep. The deeper you go, the better you will understand your customer and be able to solve their problem. What keeps them lying awake in bed at 2:00AM? What is that emotional 'hot button' that is driving them to look for the solution to their problem? Write these down with your customer avatar.

When you break this down, you need to know two categories of information:
- What do they want to *get*?
- What do they want to *avoid*?

On a separate sheet of paper, draw a line down the middle. Write, "What they want to GET," on one side and, "What they want to AVOID" on the other.

Make a *long* list. Try hard to come up with at least 15 or 20 items in each column. Remember, you are dealing with the emotional, *chimpanzee* brain, not the logical brain. After completing this list, go back and figure out the biggest hot buttons, the top 2 or 3 that have the most *emotional* impact.

To solve your customer's problem, you have to understand his or her emotional needs and wants. Step inside their head and find the actual words they use inside their *chimpanzee* mind and the experiences that trigger an unmet emotional need. The emotional, irrational chimpanzee brain has convinced them that the problem is caused by something outside of them, so they will look for a solution outside of them. Logic does not cause a person to make a buying action...only emotion does. Logic simply validates, rationalizes and supports the emotional decisions made by the illogical chimpanzee brain.

Write out a customer avatar in explicit detail. Interview existing customers. If you are a new business and don't have existing customers, you must create a survey and conduct extensive research on who will buy your product or service. Without research, you are running your business blindfolded, and it will eventually fail. Only make decisions based on <u>data</u>, not on your own chimpanzee-based intuition. Assume nothing.

Understand the emotional experience of your customers in explicit detail. What is their day-to-day routine like? What is their lifestyle? Who are the significant people in their lives? Write out their fears, frustrations, aspirations, and goals. Understand what keeps them lying awake at 2:00AM. Know precisely what they want to *get* and what they want to *avoid*. Never stop asking, "What is my customer thinking and experiencing?" Create products and services that directly address what your customer wants to GET and AVOID *emotionally*, and your products will practically sell themselves.

Footnote or Endnote:

    1. Michael E. Gerber, *The E-Myth Revisited* (New York: HarperCollins, 1995), 2.

Corresponding Bibliographical Entry:

Gerber, Michael E. *The E-Myth Revisited.* New York: HarperCollins, 1995.

Emilie Shoop is a sought after Coach, Mompreneur, Strategist, Mentor, Speaker, Author, Trainer, Business Consultant, and Creator and Leader of Shoop Training & Consulting. She is an eternal networker who never meets a stranger. With 15+ years of experience creating valuable connections, she is a Social Network Coach to entrepreneurs, direct sales professionals, teams, and organizations. Her methods help you create the connections you need to succeed!

Emilie works with people who are ready for that next level of success, and realize how they work with people is **KEY**. Her coaching will help you lead, delegate, sell, collaborate, perform, influence, and relate with people to launch your success to the next level.

One of Emilie's pet peeves is unhappy people in the work place. People are either unhappy with the work they are doing, their bosses, or their employers. It is this belief that drives her to reach out and impact others. Her coaching, speeches, workshops and seminars motivate and inspire as she involves and leads participants through dynamic transformations that enhance their ability to be focused and empowering leaders and teams.

Contact Information:

Shoop Training & Consulting
PO Box 192
Heyworth, IL 61745
www.shooptc.com
www.facebook.com/shooptc
info@shooptc.com

Chapter 11

The Art of Delegation

Emilie Shoop

The Art of Delegation, or as I like to say it, "How to ask someone to do something for you in a way that they will want to do it for you, and do it well," can seem like an art form near impossible to learn. It's hard to know when to delegate, what to say, and what to do. Every entrepreneur, regardless of how many employees there are in the company, struggles with this at some point.

Are you just starting out and figuring out that there is not enough time to do the work, marketing, customer relations, make coffee, and do the accounting?

Maybe you've hired a couple people and still have work that isn't getting done, or you feel like your business is just treading water. Or do you have a full blown staff with multiple departments and lots of work to get done?

> "Nothing is impossible if you can delegate."
>
> ~Unknown

As an unstoppable entrepreneur you will need to seek to continually delegate more and more so that you can focus on what you are good at, what you are passionate about, and what gives the customer the most benefit. This allows continuous learning, growth, and expansion of your mind to continually remain on top!

Why even bother to delegate in the first place? What should you delegate? I find it hard to separate these two questions. Why you delegate leads to what you delegate, and what you delegate leads to why you delegate.

Doing it yourself may seem easier and gives the appearance of saving money. But the key here is that it *seems* easier and cheaper, but unfortunately, that's usually not the case.

WHAT TO DELEGATE

Here is a list of tasks you could begin delegating today:

- Accounting work
- Proofreading
- Research on a pending purchase
- Ordering or purchasing supplies
- Travel arrangements
- Making and setting appointments
- Maintenance on office space
- Hardware or software installs
- Graphic design
- Event planning
- Routine customer service
- Hiring/recruiting
- Fulfilling orders
- Process incoming and outgoing mail

Are any of the above tasks filling your days so you can't move your business forward? Time to see if you could delegate them!

There are **three easy checks** to test a situation to see if it's a good time to delegate them:

1. Is it repetitive?
2. Is it what I am *really* good at?
3. Is it something that would take less time for someone else to do?

Is it repetitive?
Let's say you are working in your office and you have a task that has to be done every week. A good example would be entering expenses in your account tracking software. This is a routine and repetitive task. Once you set up the software, and train the person doing the entering how to do it, it can be done week after week with limited involvement on your part.

Again, this is something that you can easily do. It's not difficult and it's really not a big deal for you to do. However, this is a perfect opportunity to delegate.

Is it what I am REALLY good at?
Using the previous example of entering expenses in your account tracking software...unless you are an accountant or numbers are your thing, entering expenses is probably not where your strengths are. If the task at hand is part of being in business, but it is not where you shine, it's a good opportunity to delegate.

"The best executive is the one who has sense enough to pick good men to do what he wants done and slef-restraint enough to keep from meddling with them while they do it."
~ Theodore Roosevelt

As before, this is still something you could keep doing yourself, but sit back and ask yourself, "Is this a task that maximizes the use of my abilities?" If not, then delegate it!

Is it something that would take less time for someone else to do?
Now I know that it seems like it doesn't really take you that long to do some of the tasks that I suggest you delegate. However, once you really look at how much time it takes, you might see it a little differently. Take again the example of entering in your expenses. The process involves you just typing in a couple numbers, right? If you are anything like most busy entrepreneurs, it looks a little more like this:

1. Find all the receipts. Check the folder you meant to put them in, the piles on your desk, your car, your wallet, and pockets of everything you've worn since the last time you entered your receipts.
2. Try not to get distracted by other things that need your attention.
3. Open the software program you are using to record expenses. Find your password, if not have it reset (again).
4. Try not to get distracted by other things that need your attention.
5. Enter the expenses. Have you procrastinated and find that there are now weeks or months worth of receipts to catch up on?
6. Try not to get distracted by other things that need your attention.
7. Close the software program.
8. Try not to get distracted by other things that need your attention.
9. File the receipts so that you have them all in one place for tax time.
10. Done!

Delegating the task to someone else often involves a little bit of systemizing, but once it's set up, some tasks can go into auto-pilot. Your work for entering expenses, once you delegate, could go something like this:

1. Throw all receipts in a folder as they are received.
2. Hand over the folder to the person who will be entering them on the agreed upon day or time.
3. Get back to work on things that need your attention.

Now the person doing the work can have systems in place to just get the task at hand done in a minimal amount of time and you are free to do the work that is the best use of *your* time.

It's just as fast to do it myself as it is to explain it all to someone.

The biggest resistance I get from people when I suggest they delegate is that it takes too long to hand the task over to someone else. "It's just as fast to do it myself as it is to explain it all to someone else." Yes, this is usually true the first time. But as you can see above, if you are really streamlining the task, it can end up taking less time for two people to get it done than it was taking you alone.

My career has evolved over the years, and a bulk of it was spent in the world of Network Engineering. In order to troubleshoot, monitor, and deploy our network, we would end up using scripts that would automate the process. I was not a programmer and had very little training in writing scripts. As I was learning how to write the scripts, I was given some great advice from my teammates. Since it seemed so tedious and time consuming to put together a script, I had asked them why you would bother writing one. They said you should take the time to write a script when you find yourself doing the same manual task over and over, and the amount of time it took to write the code would save you the time of having to repeat the work being done. That's exactly what you need to think of when it comes time to delegate.

D.R.I.V.E.

Now that you have a task that you would like to delegate, how are you going to get someone else to do the work, and do it right? The second biggest complaint I get about delegating is that the work is not done right, not on time, or just not what they expected at all. There are **five simple steps** to drive you to delegating the right way, every time.

D·R·I·V·E·
Define
Resources
Inform
Validate
Evaluate

Define Step 1: **Define**

Define exactly what the person will be doing for you. Take a few minutes to think through all of the specifics; the more details the better. Have a clear vision and convey that to the person you are engaging. Include details such as time constraints, budgets, rules and regulations, and any other expected outcomes.

Resources
Step 2: **Resources**

Compile a list of all the resources the person will need to get the job done. Be sure to think of resources that are available to assist, but may not be mandatory to complete the job. Be as detailed and all-inclusive as possible.

Inform
Step 3: **Inform**

Have a conversation with the person you are delegating to. Describe the responsibility. Discuss possible barriers. Ask the assignee for any feedback, questions, concerns, and so on. Review his or her understanding of the expectations, and set a time to review progress.

Validate Step 4: <u>Validate</u>

When delegating, it is crucial that the person taking over the task knows that you support them, are available for questions, and believe they can get the job done for you. The more encouraging you are about the task being delegated, the better your results will be.

Evaluate

Step 5: <u>Evaluate</u>

Set up times on longer projects to check in on the progress and make sure things are progressing as planned. Open the door to allow for any corrections or changes to be made before the deadline is upon you. If it is a short task, make sure to evaluate the work and give praise and/or guidance as needed so that the next time the work is done, it's to the level you desire and expect.

There will be times, however, when you should <u>not</u> delegate. I wanted to be sure you don't get too excited about delegating, and forget there are things you actually <u>should</u> be doing.

EXAMPLE

Now let's walk through an example of using the D.R.I.V.E. steps to delegate. When I'm working with people, I like to use the following example, because it seems so simple until you really look into it. Let's say that you would like to have your employee, Joe, plan the company picnic. How would you delegate that task?

Define

Questions to flush out before you assign the task to Joe could be:

- Has it been done before? If so, is it to be like last year's or should it be different? Different how?
- Is this a family event as well, or just for employees?
- Does it take place during work hours, or at night? Will it be over the weekend?
- Should the assignee be the only one do the planning, or should there be a committee involved?
- Are there to be activities? If so, what kind?
- How much of the planning is at the assignee's discretion?
- How much can be spent?
- When should the event be…next week, next month, a specific date, a rough timeframe?
- Is it a 2, 4, or 6 hour event? How long should it be planned for?
- Does the budget include food? Are there any vegetarians or special meal accommodations that need to be addressed?
- Is entertainment to be provided? Is there budget for that?
- Is alcohol allowed?
- Where should the picnic be held? At the office? Should space be rented? A local park?
- How much work time should Joe spend on planning this?

This is not an all-inclusive list, but you can see where I began to flush out details. The more guidance you can provide, and really paint a picture of the work you are asking Joe to do, the better the results. You definitely want to give him as much authority and ability to make decisions without you doing the work, but give him parameters to work within.

One of the most important questions is how much work time should Joe spend on this task. I've worked with people who feel as if this could become their full time job; and I've worked with people who could spend a couple hours the night before pulling it together. Set boundaries, and then let Joe work within them.

Resources

Now create a list of all the resources Joe will need to get the job done. Here are questions to answer:

- Did someone plan it last year, and can Joe work with that person, or ask questions?
- Will anyone be helping Joe? If so, who?
- Are there company policies that Joe will need to adhere to? Where are those located so he can review them?
- If Joe gets stuck on finding a venue, who is a good resource to contact?
- Will Joe be using his computer, a list of preferred vendors, a printer to send out invites, an online invitation solution, etc.?
- Is there someone that works within the company, or a family member of an employee that caters, bakes, has a band, a DJ, or anything else Joe might need?

Again, this is not an all-inclusive list, but should help you get started. The mistake I see people making on this one is forgetting to let Joe know who could help even though they aren't necessarily assigned to the task. If you don't tell Joe, he might not know they could help, or that it's okay to ask for that help.

Inform Now that you have spent a few minutes gathering all the details Joe will need, it's time to delegate. Sit down and describe the responsibility to Joe and ask him how he feels about it. Discuss any possible barriers. Will his current workload allow it? Is there any reason why he wouldn't be able to do the job as you intended? Ask Joe what support is needed from you or others in the company. Review Joe's understanding and make sure it's the same as you intended. The clearer you are upfront, the better results you will get. Don't forget to set up a time to check-in along the way.

It is easy to forget to ask the person you are delegating to for their input. A lot of time and frustration can be saved by being open for feedback. Joe could be so overloaded, that it would never get done. Or, you could be asking him to do something he always wanted to and already has a list of 50 ideas ready to go. Asking for that feedback will help you make sure the task is delegated successfully.

Validate It is important that Joe knows that taking over this assignment is a compliment to his abilities and potential. Let him know that you believe in him, and that he can ask questions at any time. Here is a little secret to getting people to **want** to do work for you...tell them how much you believe in them.

Evaluate Finally, set up times with Joe to give an update on how things are coming along. This allows for any corrections, additions, changes, and so on to be made before it's too late. That sounds negative, but it's not. Joe could be doing such an amazing job finding great deals, which can stretch the company's budget. It also gives you and Joe peace of mind to know the job is on track. Nobody likes to finish a job and then find out it was wrong. Nor do you want to show up at the company picnic and it be nothing like you wanted.

THE ART OF DELEGATING

When it comes to delegating, you define the "what" and the people doing the work decide the "how." Although you take the necessary time to be clear about what should be done, you are not doing the actual work. Once you have delegated, keep out of it until help is asked of you. This is where your trust in the person doing the work takes over, and you are finally free to get more of your own work done! Use this time wisely and allow the work to get done *for* you. This can be extremely hard for many entrepreneurs, but it's the best way to get amazing results and reach the level of success you desire and deserve!

DO NOT DELEGATE

Now that you are delegating with ease, I don't want you to get carried away with it. There are things that should not be delegated, or should only be delegated with extreme caution as you grow.

- Who you are to your customer: Whether you are the creative mastermind, the technical genius, or the keen consultant, don't delegate that so you don't perform that role any more. It is okay to build your team and teach others your way, but ultimately, it is best for your business for you to have your main focus on that skill set.
- Who you are to your business:

You are the entrepreneur, the leader of your business. While you can delegate authority, don't delegate your position. Always maintain your leadership and position, so you are not causing confusion to those who work with and within your business.

- Who you are:
  It is easy to get caught up in running a business. However, be sure not to delegate your mission, vision, or values. Keep true to yourself, why you started the business, and what you stand for. Although these may evolve over time, do not let them become someone else's.

Moving forward, you are now equipped to be an unstoppable entrepreneur because you can delegate the work that consumes your time and does not allow you to focus where it really counts. The more you delegate, the happier your clients will be, the easier it will be for you to grow, and ultimately, the more successful you will be!

Elaine Bailey is the president and founder of *Elaine Bailey International Ltd* and Work*Brilliant Coaching Solutions,* a learning and development organization devoted to mentoring successful corporate leaders and inspired entrepreneurs to become the best they possibly can be by taking a whole new approach to personal development, productivity, business and lifestyle.

Elaine has created, designed and delivered internationally successful programmes and trainings that have helped 1000's of managers and senior executives step into a high level of leadership in their companies and in their teams.

Elaine's Work*Brilliant* online magazine has an international readership, sharing weekly articles, tips and advice. It has been reprinted on several world-renowned websites. She is a published author and has written a chapter in Sheri McConnell's latest book, *Smart Women Embrace Transitions* (Published on Amazon in May 2012).

Elaine's Master's Degree in Coaching and Mentoring Practice is from Oxford Brookes University. David Clutterbuck and Eric Parsloe have mentored her during her studies. In addition, Elaine is a Business Practitioner in NLP, and a Chartered MCIPD. She has studied Transactional Analysis and specialised in Psychology for her MA.

She has privately coached people in professional fields ranging from nursing, therapy, veterinary practice, law, banking to scientific research. She was the coach-mentor for Barclays Bank GRB Technology's *Maximise Your Potential* – Talent management programme from 2009 – 2011.

Contact Information:
Website: www.elainebaileyinternational.com
Email: info@elainebaileyinternational.com
LinkedIn: http://uk.linkedin.com/in/elainejbailey
Facebook: www.facebook.com/elainejbailey

Chapter 12

Learn More to Earn More –
Why Your Business Needs You to Keep Growing!

Elaine Bailey

"Learn as if you were going to live forever. Live as if you were going to die tomorrow."
Mahatma Gandhi, *Preeminent Leader of Indian Nationalism.*

When I decided to step away from the corporate world and start my own business I knew I had a lot to learn. I was fired up, excited and ready to go! I bought all the self-help business books that everyone recommended and I willingly signed up for numerous online programs and packages.

I was deadly serious about becoming a successful entrepreneur.
Then I drowned in an ocean of self-help modules, marketing books, and leadership resources. I felt overwhelmed and scared because I had so much stuff to learn. I had no plan, so the learning tools gathered dust on a shelf and I got busy *doing* the job trying to create my business and being everything for my clients!

My personal development was relegated to the bottom of my 'To-Do' list because I was too busy. I'd get stuck with basic business challenges because I didn't know what to do. Other business owners around me seemed to be growing faster and getting better results, and this hurt. I felt like I was going backwards and everything was so difficult because I had no frame of reference.

Here's what I realized…

I'd stopped learning and growing. Buying learning materials won't make you learn – You have to APPLY the tools consistently! This is where most business owners fall down.

Whatever your business, one of the minimum requirements of being successful is your ability to grow. The *future* of YOU and your business belongs to *learning*. Active continuous personal development separates a successful business owner from a mediocre one… and the gap between the two is huge!

I was trying to grow my business without growing myself. This was a recipe for failure – The success of my business starts with me - It grows from the *inside out*. If you have a static view about your business, you will get lost in the *'do-do'* of *doing* the work. This is known as working IN your business.

When you constantly work IN your business it's easy to become boxed in by limited thinking. You are focused on *doing* the job day after day and you forget something really important:

Your business is organic: It only evolves and grows if you evolve and grow. Stagnation can destroy a business. If you stop learning, then you stop growing, your business doesn't evolve, and you get left behind. You stop leading and start surviving. You become reactive rather than proactive and creative in everything you do.

I've come to recognise that personal growth is the minimum requirement for success.

If learning is so important, then why don't we ALL do it?

Learning is under-rated by many people and personal development is seen as a *'nice' to have* rather than a *'need' to have*. Instead, you rely solely on past experience and existing knowledge to solve any problems. After all, you've been successful up to now!

What you don't realize is that as the business world changes the learning gap between *what you know* and *what you need to know* gets wider. Last year's answers won't solve today's challenges because the business playing field has changed! Unconsciously, you get locked into a holding pattern of fixed thinking that reinforces any limiting beliefs associated with, "This is just how business is," or "Business is tough," or "It's hard because of the economy." These become our personal truths and we use them as excuses to stay stuck and wait for something external to change.

People who aren't learning focus only on WHAT needs to be done. When they become overwhelmed, they try to change WHAT they're doing, but they are limited because the nature of the work IS the work!

The uncertainty of "not knowing" causes fear and doubt because you want assurance that it's all going to turn out okay. You feel like you have no control over your workload and you're frightened that clients will either all flood in all at once or there will be a drought.

How to recognize if you DON'T have a learning mindset...
You've become an order taker. You just focus on *doing* the work. You never stop to look at how you're doing it. You might have lost your passion because it all feels so difficult to do. You may have left the corporate world and set up your business doing what you were previously doing as an employee – Now you're doing it for yourself. Here lies a paradox: *Some entrepreneurs run their businesses with an employee mindset rather than evolving the mindset of a business owner.*

No strategy – Just delivery. You have no real clarity or vision for your *business.* It all centers on your products or services and getting the job done. You don't have a strategy; you just react to anything that is urgent in the moment.

You don't have any systems, structures, processes or support in place to help you. Everything feels like hard work!

Not enough hours in the day. You're already so thinly spread that there is hardly enough time in the day to get everything done. How could you possibly have any time to step back and grow? You're too busy doing it all! The only option is to work harder and you feel that you are already reaching your limit.

You don't invest in your growth. You're trying to do it all on your own without any support. You're being everything to everybody. You're not developing your leadership skills to run a business. You often take advice from your friends or family, (who incidentally have never run their own business). You see learning as a luxury that you don't have time to do. You buy books but you never read them!

How to recognize if you HAVE a learning mindset...

You focus on the HOW. If something isn't working you look at HOW you do things and create new systems to help the flow. You have processes and practices that streamline your activities and save you time. You don't react and fundamentally change the nature of WHAT you're doing every time something goes wrong.

You know your high value work. You have clarity, vision and purpose: You know WHY you are in business. You're moving towards more of what you want rather than moving away from what you don't want. You're clear on your *High Value Work* (what's important) and focus your time and energy on these activities. *Low value work* is *automated*, *delegated* or *deleted*. You are selective and stay focused on what's important.

You work to a schedule. You know what you're doing BEFORE you sit down to do it. You have a weekly schedule and work according to it. You have standards and boundaries in place so that time doesn't hemorrhage away. You schedule time for marketing, personal growth, business development, and for being creative so you get to focus on your strengths and do your 'genius work.'

You're in the business of marketing. You understand the value of marketing and have created CONSISTENT *stay-in-touch* strategies with your stakeholders, clients or prospective clients. You're learning how to be a marketer and it's part of your weekly plan! You build relationships and network online and offline. You understand that marketing is EVERYTHING if you want to create a successful business.

You surround yourself with like-minded people. You invest in your own personal growth. Your learning and growth is a CONSISTENT strategy. You network and mastermind with like-minded business people. You have a coach or mentor to help you understand and develop your marketing, leverage, mindset and skills as a leader. Successful leaders are always growing and changing. Working *ON* your business gives you a whole new approach to productivity, business and lifestyle. It creates a balanced approach to your whole life.

HOW TO LEARN MORE to EARN MORE... By investing in your own personal growth...
I have been a professional learning and development consultant for 25 years. Here's my personal development success formula for business owners... You have to INVEST three key areas of need:

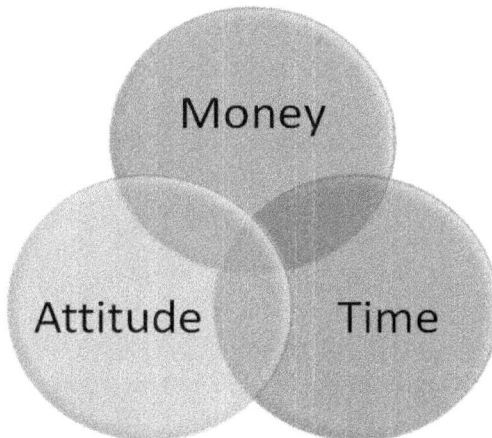

Work*Brilliant* ® Personal Development Success Formula

INVESTMENT	DETAILS
Money	Learning is both a personal and business investment. You are increasing your marketability and leverage through increasing your knowledge and capability. You can invest in many ways and it doesn't have to be expensive. You are buying the wisdom and expertise of others. Here are a few examples: Books, mentors, workshops, trainings and online resources.
Time	*Take time to make time!* Regular planning and scheduling time for personal development is extremely important. It is *High Value Work* – don't blow it off because you're *busy*! You are upgrading your knowledge and capability. This is essential for business success. Make your personal development a high priority.
Attitude	Invest in a growth mindset and take your personal development very seriously. Approach learning with a positive attitude. Be committed to making it happen. It's part of your business strategy and it's just what you do. Learning needs discipline and persistence; this is the glue to make it happen.

All three of these elements need to be satisfied because they are interconnected and inter-related. It takes a combination of all these elements to create sustainable and successful personal growth.

Successful people invest **time, money** and **attitude** in their own personal development and it pays off. They take learning seriously because they recognize its real value both personally and professionally.

Grow your own success from the *inside out*:

1. **Start from where you are now** – Don't wait for the perfect moment because it will never come. Start today. Prioritize your learning – you can't learn everything at once! You may have loads of books, online workshops, or learning resources that are waiting on a dusty shelf. Just choose ONE. Work through that one resource then move on to the next.

2. Be committed NOT interested - Once you have set your intention, then you *have to* make a 100% commitment to learning if you really want it to happen! If you are only interested in learning, you'll only learn when it is convenient, which might not be very often.

Here's what 100% commitment looks like:

- You are committed to learning and there are *no excuses,* only results.
- You have discipline – It's just part of your daily **practice**.
- You've made the decision – You're committed to making it happen and you don't have to think about it anymore. The decision has been made – You're doing it!
- You observe the boundaries you've made to make this happen.
- You show up every day despite obstacles and not feeling like it no matter what the circumstances.

3. Read for an hour a day – Wake up an hour earlier and read first thing each morning. If you do this 5 days a week, that's five hours of reading. Just think of how many books you could read in a year and the advantage you would have over your competition! You'd be the expert. Make notes and apply one thing you've read during the day. Start with 30 minutes and build your time up. Turn off the television and read for an hour each night (especially if you "don't do" mornings).

4. Listen to audio books on the move – I listen to learning materials while I'm working out at the gym. I find the gym boring. Now, I learn as I workout and time flies by. I make a few notes back in the changing room. You can also listen as you drive, fly, or take the train. Turn traveling time into learning time.

5. Have the right ATTITUDE for learning – Is your passion for what you do greater than any inconvenience it may cause? I travel thousands of miles for my own personal development and it's not always convenient. I look beyond discomfort because I'm passionate about being the best I can possibly be. Get out from behind the convenience of your computer and look beyond the discomfort of traveling. Take your personal development seriously by activity; seek out specific events and trainings that will help you grow. Group learning can expand your mind and ability. Go to the source of the expertise and learn from the best if you want to be the best!

6. Plan your personal development time – Schedule dates and times for learning in advance and show up for it! Personal development time is now HIGH VALUE WORK. It's essential for your business development. Look for opportunities to learn – carry a book, an iPad or kindle with you. Read while you wait for appointments instead of seeing it as wasted time.

7. Apply what you learn – Acquiring knowledge is only a small part of the process. USING what you've learned is when growth really happens and it's critical for success. Many entrepreneurs that I know can reel off an impressive list of business books that they've read but only about 10% have actually applied any of the content to their daily lives. You have to be disciplined to make it happen. Look for opportunities to practice what you've learned as soon as possible.

8. Work with a mentor – If you want to run a six-figure business, then you need to learn from someone who has had first-hand experience of achieving your goal and can provide the wisdom, intuition and support. Working one on one will help you to stay focused, be accountable, keep your commitment and create the discipline and persistence to make things happen. The right mentor can help you to grow beyond recognition and become a bigger and more successful version of yourself. It's like having an extra director on your team.

If you want to earn more, you have to learn more! Learning is not just a one time and done event, it's a constant throughout your life. Are you passionate enough about your success to INVEST in your personal development?

Recommended Reading and Resources

http://www.elainebaileyinternational.com/wordpress/blog/   Free weekly advice – Elaine Bailey -Work*Brilliant*® -Weekly eZine

http://www.amazon.com - Smart Women Embrace Transition

In 15 years as a paramedic, trainer, manager, and dispatcher in emergency services, Karen kept cool under pressure and learned to make a wide range of good decisions, fast. Next, as a senior manager in the public service, Karen received awards for innovation and excellence. Today, as co-owner of a results-based coaching firm and a certified NLP Master Coach and Master Hypnotist, Karen brings all her skills into play. Her extraordinarily ability to relate to a wide range of people, her ability to react on the spot, and her studies in NLP (neuro-linguistic programming) and hypnosis help her clients make the changes they long for. Fast.

Today Karen and her partner Jeff are busy building a results-based coaching firm that empowers clients to choose real results over out-dated reasons. ChooseRESULTS provides individual coaching, couples coaching, executive coaching for new managers and entrepreneurs, and personal effectiveness training. Training courses (in-house and online) include: *Confident Decision Making*; *Goal Setting for Results*; *Neuro Linguistic Programming* (NLP) at the Practitioner and Master levels; and *Hypnosis*.

Karen is often asked to share her experience in personal effectiveness and project management at events and conferences. She is an experienced and engaging speaker, available for keynote addresses, conferences, webinars, and workshops.

Keep your reasons or...
ᚴCHOOSERESULTS

401 Logan Ave, Unit 206A
Toronto, ON M4M 2P2
647.343.0664
KKessler@ChooseRESULTS.ca
www.ChooseRESULTS.ca

Chapter 13

Confident Decision Making

Karen Kessler

Does making big decisions for your business keep you up at night? Do you need an easier way to make great decisions every time? Looking for confidence in the face of uncertainty?

In this chapter I will share one decision making technique that works for me and the many that have taken my Confident Decision Making course.

You will learn:
- How to tell a decision from a problem or dilemma
- One easy decision making process that can be scaled to meet your needs
- How to identify and avoid pitfalls and traps that pull decision making off track

Confident decision making is the hallmark of every successful entrepreneur. Mastering the system in this chapter will raise your confidence and decision making skill. With better decisions come more success, and less risk for you and your business.

Entrepreneurs come from all walks of life. Yet each one I meet reflects on the sheer number of decisions to be made not only during start-up, but throughout the life of their business. Do any of these look familiar?

- Where do I set up shop? Should I own or lease?
- Who is my ideal client going to be?
- Do I source product(s) in this country or overseas?
- Should I advertise? If so, how, where and how much?
- Is it time to ask for help? How much am I willing to pay for coaching or mentoring?
- What funding option(s) will best serve me now and into the future?

If you don't have experience in making big decisions without a net, you are not alone. Many entrepreneurs either come from jobs within a hierarchy where someone else owns the final decision.

But…remember that you have managed your life and made lots of decisions up to this point, including the one to join our ranks as an entrepreneur. As your experience grows, the alternatives or options can come easily and decisions seem to make themselves. What do we do when the subject matter changes and we feel out of our element? That's when we fall back to a system we can count on until our experience and knowledge catches up.

To start, I'd like to share with you some of the *bad* decisions that I've made that have had painful consequences lasting for ten or more years. My careers, before embracing entrepreneurship, were in public service and private enterprise and they shaped my decision making process – the scars even more than the good decisions! Today, my confidence comes from knowing what works, what doesn't, and how to manage myself when emotions or the stakes run high.

While my use of this Confident Decision Making system becomes less formal over time, any key decisions that I make still get the full treatment. I have worked too hard to build my business to have it sidetracked by my ego.

I'm now full-time and committed to my Professional Results Coaching company. There simply is no room for failure.

However, there is always room for mistakes. Making good decisions creates a buffer and opportunities to make further decisions down the road as more information becomes available. This flexibility gives me space to breath and great sleep at night. With my process, you too can become a confident decision maker and an unstoppable entrepreneur.

Let's get started.

You will need a pencil, pad of paper and a decision you would like to make today. Watch for the '**Action**' statements for directions on applying the system to your own decision. Taking the opportunity to apply the system to an actual decision as you read through the chapter will provide a much better learning experience.

How to tell if it's a decision

Decisions, Problems, and Dilemmas all require a different tactical approach. Knowing how to tell them apart is the first step to becoming a confident decision maker.

Make Decisions
Do you have a number of alternatives or options to choose from?
Do you have clear objectives necessary for a good outcome?
Do you have the knowledge and authority to make the choice?

If you find yourself asking the above questions, then it's a decision.

An example would be cash flow funding – there are several options to consider when funding is required: loan, credit, house loan. All are viable and will meet your needs.

Alex Lowy in his book, *No Problem,* explains how the level of complexity and uncertainty determines how to approach any given situation (see Figure 1).

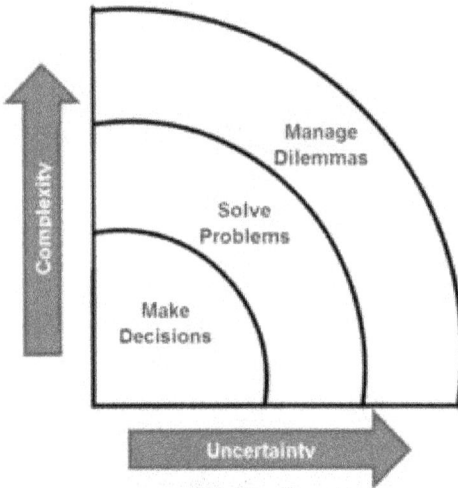

Figure 1

Solve Problems

Problems have higher uncertainty and complexity than decisions. You will spot these when the solution is not immediately obvious but you are quite certain there is one.

A good example would be when your competition drops their prices. How do you lower costs? You know there must be a way to maintain quality and pay less per unit.

Manage Dilemmas

Dilemmas lie at the far reaches of the complexity and uncertainty graph, where there is no single solution that will eliminate the issue. Often more than one solution is required. You are left making the best of the situation and looking for opportunities to benefit.

For example, in society, homelessness is a dilemma. Governments create strategies that contain many solutions to manage the issue because the dilemma is so complex.

Entrepreneurs rarely face anything so insurmountable. However, it can feel like you are when you are growing and the administrative work builds along with the business development. You will see that is most likely a decision.

Decision Making System

Step 1: Write it down! It may seem like a simple step, but clarity is essential and putting your decision down on paper will make sure you are clear.

Action: Write your decision in a single sentence that includes the options you are considering. See examples below.

_____

_____

_____

_____

Examples:
My business has grown and now requires administrative support. I am thinking about filling the gap with a virtual assistant, an intern from the local college, or hiring a relative/close friend.

-Or-

My business requires a website for customers to learn more about me and my services. I could build my own, hire a firm to design and build the site, or do without for now.

Step 2: Select the Objectives – what is important about the outcome? Is it total cost, time invested, impact to your client/customer, or maybe how much recognition you will receive? These are high level objectives or criteria that each option will be evaluated against.

Start with brainstorming to flush out any possible objective that may not be obvious. Take 60 seconds and jot down everything that comes to mind in the space below.

Action: Brainstorm about what is important to you about the outcome of the decision.

_____   _____
_____   _____
_____   _____
_____   _____
_____   _____

Action: Review the results and circle the top three. If you find that there are more, consider whether there is a higher-level objective that will cover both.

Action: From the previous objectives, place the most important in the line below marked 'Objective 1,' then next most important in the 'Objective 2' space, leaving the last space for your third objective.

The final step in the objective selection is weighting.

Weighting means assigning a number to an objective in relation to its importance; the higher the number, the greater the weight, and the greater influence on outcome.

Examples:

	Weight
Objective 1 – <u>Overall cost per year</u>	<u>x1</u>
Objective 2 – <u>Aligns to values</u>	<u>x3</u>
Objective 3 – <u>My time and effort</u>	<u>x2</u>

Or,

	Weight
Objective 1 – <u>Effect on reputation</u>	<u>x2</u>
Objective 2 – <u>Opportunity to leverage</u>	<u>x1</u>
Objective 3 – <u>Boosts profits</u>	<u>x2</u>

If all of your selected objectives are equally important to you, no weighting is required.

Action: Fill in the weight for each objective below.

Weight

Objective 1 _____   _____
Objective 2 _____   _____
Objective 3 _____   _____

Step 3: Alternatives – Having a number of alternatives, also called options, is what made this a decision in the first place. The quality of the decision can be measured by the range, quality, and wording of alternatives you are considering. Let's cover each of these separately.

Range of Alternatives
Writing down the obvious options is a great place to start. But don't stop there!

Take the time to consider other alternatives that may serve your needs. This will reduce your bias towards your first impression and allow for some innovative decision making.

Embrace the ridiculous. I always push the envelope when looking for inspiration. Ask yourself these questions:

1. What would happen if ...
2. What am I assuming?
3. What would be the craziest way to do this?

The point is to shake up the "thought rut" you might be in. Sometimes the entire nature of the decision changes when you find non- traditional alternatives.

I have made loads of decisions that made other people scratch their heads. Many have turned out to provide huge paybacks.

Be sure to use all the resources available to you. Mentors, people in a similar business, and your entrepreneur networks may all have alternatives for you to consider.

Remember the status quo – what would happen if you left everything just as it is for now? If this is a viable alternative, then I recommend including it. It is also a great way to see just how much better the other alternatives really are once you get to scoring.

Quality of Alternatives
Would you honestly implement the decision if the alternative scored highest? If the option isn't viable, then don't include it in the process.

Action: Gather as many options as possible, make them varied, extreme, and even include the status quo. Then sift, sort and separate the three you would consider implementing.

Alternative: _____

_____

Alternative: _____

_____

Alternative: _____

_____

Wording
Tweak the wording of the three alternatives chosen.

Action: Remove all bias and opinion from the words leaving a clear tagline to represent the alternative.

The bias adds no value and will affect the scoring in a way that could lead to a poor decision. If it really is the best alternative, then *trust the process* and it will come out ahead. The short clear tagline will fit in the table easily.

Examples:
Instead of 'Move business across town to the busiest intersection,' use 'Move business to 181 Center Street.'

-Or-

Instead of 'Impersonal financial services from one of the big banks' use, 'Financial Services at 'bank of X.''

Action: Write your new bias-free taglines in the space provided

Alternative tagline: _____
Alternative tagline: _____
Alternative tagline: _____

Step 4: The Decision – Let's do the math. Scoring each alternative against the objectives allows you to thoroughly measure the validity of each course of action you are considering for this decision.

Review the sample, and then follow the action steps to score your own decision.

The sample table below (see figure 2) shows the placement of the information. .

	Objective 1 (weight)	Objective 2 (weight)	Objective 3 (weight)	Totals
Alternative 1				
Alternative 2				
Alternative 3				

Figure 2: Sample Decision Making Table

Example: Business cards
For this decision the *objectives* are:

Professional Quality – These cards will represent my business and need to be quality recycled paper with great color. Weight (x2)

Cost per unit – The initial price might seem low, but once all miscellaneous fees are added in, what does it really cost per card? Weight (x1)

Flexibility in volume – If your business cards change often, printing a small number might be wise. Conversely, if you have a trade show you will want to print in larger volumes. For this decision it's about larger volumes (Weight x1)

Here is the example in the Decision Table (see Figure 3)

Decision: Business Cards	Professional Quality (x2)	Cost per Unit (x1)	Volume Flexibility (x1)	Totals
Print my own				
On-line vendor				
Local Printer				

Figure 3: Example Ready for Scoring

The *Alternatives* for this decision are:

Print My Own – Using my own color printer, ink, and purchasing a kit from the local office supply store.

On-line Vendor – I have researched some on-line business card printers and found one I would consider ordering from if it proves to be the best alternative. I will use their pricing and information for scoring this decision.

Local Printer – Someone I met at a networking event had great cards and I would consider using her printer as the business is local to me as well.

Here is the example completed in the Decision Table (Figure 4)

Decision: Business Cards	Professional Quality (x2)	Cost per Unit (x1)	Volume Flexibility (x1)	Totals
Print my own	3 x2 = 6	3 x1 =3	2 x1 =2	11
On-line vendor	5 x2 = 10	5 x1 = 5	5 x1 =5	(20)
Local Printer	5 x2 = 10	4 x1 = 4	5 x1 =5	19

Figure 4: Example - Complete

Action: Transfer your decision in Step 1 to the space provided in the top left corner of the table.

Action: Write in your objectives with the weighting in brackets to the first row of the table.

Action: Add your alternatives to the first column in the table (in no particular order).

Action: Complete the table one objective at a time.
For each objective consider how well each alternative meets your needs in this area. Use a **scale of 1 to 5** with 5 meaning that the objective would be fully met.

Action: Update the score in each box by multiplying it with weighting assigned to that objective and writing it in brackets beside the original score.

Action: Total the bracketed numbers in each alternative, place the number in the last column marked *Totals* and circle the highest number.

Now it's your turn. Follow these action steps to complete your own decision table (see Figure 5).

Decision:	Objectives			Totals
	(x __)	(x __)	(x __)	
Alternatives				

Figure 5: Your Practice Table

Step 5: Evaluate your decision.

Consider your reaction to the results. Are you surprised? Does it make sense? If it feels right and you can see yourself implementing that alternative with confidence, then you are complete.

However, if you think something isn't right, consider that the outcome of the decision table is only as good as the input. Was an objective or alternative missed?

Also, are two scores very close? In this case I would argue you can pick either one.

Finally consider whether or not you have fallen into a common decision making trap – review the Eight Common Barriers to Great Decision Making below.

<u>Eight Common Barriers to Great Decision Making</u>

1. Lack of Process – Using your dart board for decision making works well when no one can agree where to go to dinner, but your business is important and gaining success is worth some time and structure to consistently make good decisions.
2. Deferring to an expert – When in a new situation, it can be easy to just trust whatever the expert has to say. Remember that you are the only one who knows your business. I always seek out three 'experts' when getting quotes for services, or advice on high impact decisions. In the end, trust yourself.
3. Perfection – You won't sleep at night working for perfection. Consistently make effective decisions and watch for when corrections or tweaks need to be made. You will make more progress and feel more in control of your business.

4. Drowning in Information – Learn when enough is enough. Addiction to data is a real time-waster that will leave you frustrated and stuck because your business isn't moving in any direction. Malcolm Gladwell in his book, *Blink,* suggests that we learn to recognize when we have enough information to prevent paralysis.

5. Anchoring – Experts agree that it is easy to be influenced more strongly by our first impressions or by the opinions of others. Take the time to review a range of alternatives to be sure you have discovered any blind spots you may have.

6. Fear of change – Often it can feel less stressful to stay with the status quo and defend it by exaggerating the cost and discomfort of change. When success is important to you and your vision is strong, you will have the courage to consider new and different things to succeed.

7. Sticking with a losing course of action – Sometimes we have invested so much time, energy, and money, that the thought of giving up or taking a different course of action can seem unthinkable. To avoid this, seek out opinions of people not involved in the past and challenge your own motives.

8. Cherry-picking evidence – When we really like an alternative, it is common to only speak to people or listen to arguments that support your decision. To avoid this, ask neutral questions and purposely seek out opinions from people who will have another point of view.

Summary

Consistently make decisions with this process and you will find your confidence growing with each one.

Decision making is the number one skill that affects how successful you are as an entrepreneur. This is your business, your vision, and your future. Spend some time to develop your decision making skill, learn from each decision you make, and be unstoppable!

To your magnificence,
Karen

Resources and Recommended Reading
No Problem, Alex Lowy, ISBN 1425996019

Blink, Malcolm Gladwell, ISBN 0316172324

www.ConfidentDecisionMaking.com for templates, tips, and more.

Joe and Luz Adams have owned and operated several successful home businesses in the wellness, nutritional and travel industries over the last 20 years. Luz and Joe are the owners of Integrated Holistic Concepts®. They have been happily married for 17 years and currently enjoy living in Orlando, Florida.

Luz N. Adams, RN, BSN, MS, CMC, is a clinical educator, Master Coach, published author, motivational speaker, instructor and counselor, consultant, and registered nurse with thirty years of success as a driving force in healthcare and health education.

Luz is also a Reiki Master, a clinical hypnotherapist, a past life regression therapist, and a spiritual instructor (Free Soul Organization). She holds certifications as a health and wellness coach, spiritual coach, NLP coach, group coach, life coach, and master coach. She has created workshops, classes, and retreats for health care providers and the public. She is bilingual in English and Spanish.

Joe Adams is a Business and IT Professional. After careers in Sales, Retail, and Restaurant Management, Joe has spent the last 20 years in Information Technology as an Architect and Engineer designing and implementing enterprise technologies that help organizations achieve maximum benefit from their IT infrastructure. Joe is also a Reiki practitioner, Clinical Hypnotherapist, and Marketing Expert.

Luz is a charismatic team builder, passionate about bringing out the best in people. She is dedicated to help people achieve their goals and dreams through coaching, EFT, Reiki, Integrative Health Modalities, travel, and business. Luz and Joe help people build their own travel, coaching, and Integrative Health businesses. Joe is Luz's biggest supporter and the love of her life.

Integrated Holistic Concepts®
800-330-9398
Luz@IntegratedHolisticConcepts.com
www.IntegratedHolisticConcepts.com

Chapter 14

Marketing Your Business

Luz & Joe Adams

Successful marketing is the process of understanding what your customer wants, capturing your customer's attention, generating interest by appealing to their emotions, and delivering a compelling message that motivates them to buy your product or service. It's also so much more than that. Successful marketing is benefit driven, emotionally based, and laser targeted. But where do you start? We're going to give you a place to start, review some basic concepts, look at some core tools, examine some marketing strategies, and offer a few tips to be successful.

Target Marketing

The marketing process begins with understanding your ideal customer. You may also refer to them as your *specific audience.* How can you deliver an effective message without understanding who it's being delivered to? Who is your ideal customer? What motivates them to buy? What needs are they trying to satisfy? What problem can you solve for them? You want to deliver your message with laser focus to the small set of people who are ready, willing and able to buy from you – who really are excited about your product or service. You want to solve their problem and deliver results.

Start a marketing journal, notebook, or file to collect this information – it is priceless. Make a list of the characteristics that make up your best customers. Are they young, old, affluent, families, single, male, female, technically savvy, local, or national? What emotional need are they looking to satisfy? Do they want to be younger, thinner, fitter, or sexier? Do they want to do things quicker and easier, be safer, richer, or happier? These are the emotional factors you must appeal to. Your biggest payoff will be the time and energy spent clearly defining your target market.

Features vs. Benefits

Understand the difference between features and benefits. It has often been said, features (facts) tell while benefits (stories) sell. People buy benefits – they don't buy the stainless steel in the pot, they buy the fact that it is easy to clean and will last a lifetime. Make a list of benefits for your product or service. When you discover a new benefit, add to this list. Rank the benefits in order of importance to your best customers. This will help you develop your message with your key benefits targeting your best customers.

Many inexperienced marketers list fact after fact about their product, hoping that the customer will guess the benefits. Customers are too busy and distracted to make the effort. Lay out the benefits in a clear message so the customer gets it right away, and do so repeatedly throughout your marketing message. For example, if you are offering massage therapy, it's not in your best interest to advertise getting a massage. Instead, lead with the symptoms that people are experiencing like aching muscles, fatigue, stiff neck, and tension. Now you're speaking to something that's very real to them in the "now." You must inspire your customers to move into action by letting them know that you understand and _can resolve_ their immediate complaint.

Modeling is a great way to learn fast. Marketing Trainers suggest you watch infomercials to get a feel for the sequencing of "Benefit, Benefit, Benefit, and Call to Action." See if this doesn't sound familiar: "With the AB-Fantastic Gym, you will quickly and easily lose the ugly flab, have boundless energy, and feel fantastic! You will be thinner, feel younger and healthier, and look so good your friends will be asking what you have been up to - all from the comfort of your home. Call now!" Reread that slowly: Notice the emotional appeal of the benefits. See how the language makes someone say, "Yes, I need that machine."

USP – Why you?

It is important to establish your Unique Selling Proposition (USP). This answers the question of why you're the best person to buy from. "Most people look at this USP as common 'branding - why you are unique; your focus should be POSITIONING. Why you are the best, better than the rest (Mike Lewitz)." You are better because you are the "Expert", because you have deep experience in the customer's world, or because they like you and have established a relationship with you. In your message, imply reasons that make you the most preferred source for your product or service.

Marketing Plan & Budget

To be effective, you need a plan and a budget. Keep it simple, only a 2-3 page outline to start. Add it to your marketing journal or file. List your target market, your key benefits, and your USP. List what separates you from your competition. List the types of marketing you want to use for your product or service (below). List an action plan (schedule) to begin testing your marketing. List your marketing budget and outline how you want to allocate it to different approaches. Google "Marketing Plan" for examples. You will be much more efficient with a simple plan and basic budget to stay focused and manage costs.

Marketing Tools

We understand our specific audience and how to use emotionally appealing, benefit laden marketing. We have a plan and a budget. How do we get a message in front of our customers? There are some core tools to develop. They begin with the sales letter.

Sales Letter

The sales letter describes the key benefits of your product or service to your target market with emotional appeal. It can be delivered in many forms. Once written and tested, the sales letter is used to craft other sales tools by reformatting and adapting the contents. For example, the sales letter is formatted in plain text to create an email sales letter that can be emailed. The sales letter is formatted in bullets, small blocks of text, and graphics to populate your website's landing page. Spend the time to get the sales letter as powerful as possible, and then use it to develop the other tools. A good sales letter is key.

The sales letter is developed from the information you collected in your Marketing Journal. It describes the benefits of your product or service – specifically for your target market, in emotional language. Mostly focus on benefits, mention features only when necessary. The most important thing the sales letter does is tell the customer what's in it for them.

To write the sales letter, you may find it easier to simply tell a story about your product or service, as if speaking to your good friend. If writing comes easy, pretend to write your friend a letter. If speaking comes easier, get a tape recorder and tell your friend the story while recording it. Then, transcribe the tape into a letter. Edit that down, not for correct grammar, but to tell a great story.

Start with a one page letter. In our busy times, it's often better to condense down the best material into a short piece. One page will also make it easier to adapt the sales letter to other tools. For an effective sales letter, use rich, illustrative, emotional appealing language that makes your friend say, "I have to have that – I want it - Where can I get it?"

Website

Start with a simple website. You can evolve it over time. "GoDaddy.com" is one self-service site where you can cheaply build a simple website or you can hire a professional, but stay involved in the decision making. The main function of the website is to make it easier for your customer to buy your product or service. Use your sales letter to provide content about your products and services to motivate your customer to buy. Provide articles or ebooks to establish your credibility as the "expert" and set yourself apart from your competition. Use "PayPal.com" or "Clickbank.com" to provide a shopping storefront, if applicable.

Your website should help to establish a relationship with your customer to keep them coming back for more. Host a blog on your site to provide information on your product so that you become an important information resource for your customer. Provide video information and an e-newsletter to keep your customers informed about new developments or timely issues. Engage and strengthen the win-win relationship with your customer by providing value so they think only of you as their preferred supplier.

My good friend Kathy Rose is an Astrologer. She has done an excellent job of combining these elements (products, services, information, resources, expert credibility, relationship, e-newsletter, and video marketing) on "RoseAstrology.com." Whether you believe in astrology or not, take a minute to review how an effective website is put together. Adapt these concepts to your product or service. What value can you offer your customers to keep them engaged and coming back for more? Make notes in your journal or file.

Business Cards

You need them. Check out "VistaPrint.com" for inexpensive business stationary products. Also, it's wise to select the option of having the back of the card blank or with more of your business information. Do not choose the business cards advertising the stationary's company on the backside. It may be a cheaper option, but it gives the impression that you can't afford simple business cards. Pay the extra $10-$15 to make a good impression. More importantly, develop a 15-second branding statement and qualifying question to use with everyone you meet. Consider this example: "Hi, I'm Mary with Mary Smith Travel. As a Disney Certified Agent and Mother of three, I help families create those magical moments and make vacation memories that last a lifetime. Where are you planning on going for your next vacation?" Be sure to get their name and number to follow-up. Word of mouth marketing starts with you.

Brochures & Flyers
Use your sales letter to create a brochure and a one page flyer to market your product or service in public places. Include a coupon or incentive to test the effectiveness. Offer a free consultation via phone or email, or a 10% off coupon on your brochure or flyer. If people are not redeeming the incentive, refine your message.

Post Cards
You can present a highly targeted message with a post card in a direct mail piece. The good thing about direct mail is the ability to scale into large numbers. Selecting a highly targeted list is key. Once you have tested and proven a direct mail piece against a targeted mailing list (Google "Mailing Lists") you can know about how many responses to expect. Do larger mailings when you have a postcard offer that has been tested and proven to work. Duplicate that result across geography or over time. Repeat a few times annually to keep business coming in and bring new customers into your system.

Lead Lists & Databases

Both leads and your customer database are vital elements in your marketing strategy. You will need to scale up to large numbers to really enjoy big success. With direct mailing, you will want to buy leads. Laser target your leads mercilessly. Marketing costs money, so you have to get the right list. Also, know that "Business Opportunity Seekers" are generally worthless. Don't get tricked into paying more than pennies per lead. Start small and test until you get the right list.

The best lead you will ever have is one you create yourself: your customer database and prospect database. Once you have established a relationship and delivered value to a customer, it is vastly easier to sell them more of your products or services than to go find a new customer. Have a strategy for repeat business, up selling of additional products or services, and selling complementary products or services. Periodically market to your existing customers. Develop a strategy; add it to your journal and calendar. Don't over communicate or you will get tuned out, but touch base with your customers a few times a year to stay fresh in their minds. Always ask for referrals and suggest they tell a friend.

The same holds true for your prospect list. If you are providing an e-newsletter, blog or video marketing, then you are capturing the contact information of people who have expressed interest in your product. Provide compelling offers to them periodically, with specials, discounts, and other incentives to entice them to try you out. Offer a money back guarantee: they build huge credibility and very few redeem them. Develop a consistent strategy for returning to your prospects and customers over time to offer them the opportunity for more.

Marketing Strategies

We have the target market defined, the message created, and the tools created to deliver that message. What methods will get the message in front of the customer? Think scale and large numbers. Too often, we simply market to too few people.

Direct Mail

Direct Mail is experiencing a return in popularity. It is highly repeatable if your product or service fits the model. If you are a massage therapist, you can't really drive across country to give a massage. But if you create a book (or eBook) for massage to reduce stress, you can market that product in South Carolina or California. Use a highly targeted mailing list, test and tune the offer. Consider outsourcing product fulfillment.

Classified Advertising – Magazines and Newspapers

Conventional media advertising is in rapid decline. Frankly, there are better ways to spend your marketing dollars. However, in a highly targeted publication, with a proven ad, this is one way to reach large numbers of your target market. Classified advertising is fading fast, but evaluate its use in your marketing campaign.

Trade Shows

If your business is local and just starting up, then trade shows are a good way to meet large numbers of prospects. Only attend when highly targeted to your market. If you are a wedding photographer, a bridal show is a good choice, but a home and garden show may not be. Here are some quick tips:

- Use a display with limited text in large font as people don't take time to read.
- Keep the table simple so you can focus on relationships. You have 15-30 seconds to talk, so practice your branding statement and qualifying question.
- Have a "free drawing" for a product sample or splashy gift basket. Direct everyone to enter. This gives you a chance to

follow-up later with everyone. Say, "Sorry you were not the grand prize winner, but you won the second prize - a free 15 minute consultation."

- Hand everyone a flyer (cheap) with your website and contact information developed from your sales letter. It's a rapid fire event where you try to get a copy in everyone's hand and collect as many names as possible. Remember: the fortune is in the follow-up.

Online Marketing

Online marketing is somewhat complex and is constantly changing. You do want a good website to serve as a focal point for your marketing. However, more advanced concepts like Search Engine Optimization (SEO), keyword loading, and pay per click advertising can get complicated and expensive quickly. It's hard to effectively compete with the big players and the learning curve is substantial. This is one area where you may need to hire someone who already has already mastered this type of marketing.

Two types of online marketing worth the time to develop some skill are video marketing (YouTube) and blogs. The goal is to establish a "tribe" with you as "chief" (Seth Godin). By offering a blog (an online Journal), focused on your product or service, and by providing useful and valuable content (advice & resources), you set yourself up as the "expert" and deliver value to your potential customer. Answer questions, offer how-to advice and highlight trends. When combined with video, you develop a multi-media relationship that is very engaging and easy for your customer to consume. Local public access stations and colleges have eager students who need practice subjects at affordable rates to produce video.

Mobile Marketing

Mobile Marketing is an exciting new marketing strategy. Consider making this a key part of your marketing strategy for the next few years. Basically, like you used to send marketing emails to people's inbox, now you send marketing text messages to people's phones. Why the change? The majority of unsolicited email (estimated at 85%) goes unopened and unread, while the majority of text messages get opened in the first four minutes. Texts get read, email does not.

With Mobile Marketing, you invite Customers to text a "Keyword" to a "Short Code" (i.e. Text **CoachedByLuz** to 58203). Once received, the system sends a response and captures the sender's cell phone number in the customer database. Cell phone numbers rarely change which means the customer is "sticky" or stays with you in the database. You can use several types of marketing campaigns. A "drip" campaign will send out 3-7 texts over a several week period to prompt the customer to call for information, visit the website, or take some action. A "coupon" campaign will offer an incentive to be redeemed when the customer takes action. Restaurants use coupons for a free appetizer or 10% off to drive traffic on slow nights. Chiropractors, Dentists, and hair salons use mobile marketing to remind customers of appointment times and to offer an up sell incentive (i.e. 25% Off a Manicure with a Hair Cut). How can you adapt offers to your product or service?

Mobile Marketing services charge to setup the service and register the keyword. You pay for "text credits" used to send the response messages, muck like the number of minutes on your cell phone plan. You can use "viral marketing," meaning a person can forward the text to a friend. Most systems will capture each cell number in the database as the viral message is forwarded. Mobile marketing is trendy and in high growth. Take some time to get familiar with mobile marketing and see how it fits your business.

Free Publicity:
Using Free Publicity is a powerful technique to market your business. Use press releases for public radio\TV and local papers to

both provide publishable content and to offer interviews. Use the material from your sales letter. As a condition of using the material, ask for mention of your website or phone number to drive traffic. Free publicity should be a component of your marketing strategy. Add it to your journal.

What Actually Works?

It depends. These are some ideas to get you started quickly and inexpensively. Some success factors are applicable to every business. Your marketing strategy needs to be tailored to your specific audience and your product or service. Using a highly targeted, emotionally based, benefit driven marketing message that is compelling and persuasive while working to establish long term, mutually beneficial relationships with your customer is a winning formula for marketing success. The old standards of direct mail, and the emerging trends of blogs, video marketing, and mobile marketing should be evaluated to see if they fit your product or service. My good friend and marketer, Mike Lewitz, has summarized the process well: "Understand what your customer wants, figure out the emotional triggers, build [deliver] what they want, create a message that leverages those emotional triggers and entice them to buy …in that order. That's the proven model to get consumers to chase you to the ends of the Earth. …now GO take action!" (MikeLewitz.com) Ultimately, you must develop your marketing strategy and take action to build your successful business.

When do I start?

Start now. Grab a notebook and begin to define your customer and your target market. Work on your sales letter. Jot down an outline of a marketing plan and set aside a budget. Prepare some small batches of test marketing based on your sales letter. Consider them a proto type and see how they respond. Begin to populate your customer and prospect database. Test and refine your marketing campaigns. Start small; enhance what is working, scale up the successes, and scale up to larger and larger numbers. Educate yourself with marketing training: Joe Vitale, Tracy Biller, Nightengale.com, and others. Many of the techniques from their training have filtered through to be presented here. Learn, grow, and succeed. From the bottom of our hearts: Best wishes for your success!

Theo Bland is a young entrepreneur from the South-Side of Chicago. Theo Attended Hyde Park Academy and Studied Radio/TV Broadcasting at The Illinois Center for Broadcasting as well as Speech and Political Science at Chicago State University. He is a Veteran of the United States Marine Corps. Former Affiliate Producer for the former Nationally Syndicated Doug Banks Morning Show! Also, former Afternoon Drive Host of "The Stress Free House Par Tee" as well as Night and Overnight Host for several stations across different markets including Chicago.

Currently, Theo is the signature Imaging Voice for several radio stations and Syndicated Radio Programs such as "Redding News Review" and The Allison Slade Show. Mr. Bland One of the many Voices that we hear from day to day on Radio and Television promoting concerts, national stage plays and products that we all attend or consume. Theo dedicates his life to helping others achieve their dreams and goals, by offering his expertise in the areas of Media Consulting, Production, Business Building and this summer Theo Bland Voice Inc. will release the first recorded live training event called, "Activating Your Success Gene!"

Other books and Materials by Theo Bland include: The New Cheese: A Guide to Thrive in the New Economy, The Active Driver: A Guide to Drive for LIFE, The Magic of Mentoring: You Don't Know What You Don't Know, Setting and Reaching Goals: Success Is Not By Chance, It's By Choice, You Too Can Do Voice Overs: Turn Your Voice Into Money

To learn more about Theo Bland or get your copy of Theo's latest books and materials log onto:
www.TheoBlandOnline.info
www.TheoBlandVoice.com

Chapter 15

Magnificent Magic of Mentorship

Theo Bland

"Ignorance is more expensive than education."
– Donald Trump

As I navigate the journey to success, I am reminded that I never have to journey alone. In fact, it's actually highly recommended that I receive help from experts along the way. When we think of opportunities to launch new products or services or even get involved with corporate mergers and acquisitions, some common ideas come to mind relative to financing those endeavors. We think of OPM (other people's money) as a way to leverage the risk involved in our entrepreneurial endeavors and, certainly, using OPM can be a wise and cost effective way to reach those goals. We also use OPT (other people's time) as a way to leverage maximum production output, and by doing so, we increase our income as leaders. There is another principal of which I have become even fonder: OPE (other people's experience). Most people, learned or unlearned, will agree that experience is one of, if not the best of teachers. I would alter that statement slightly to say that the best teacher is one with experience. I like to call this principal the Magnificent Magic of Mentorship.

Young people who are brash and full of confidence tend to ask, "Why do I need a mentor?" This question reveals that they are idealists at heart and, without a mentor, it may take them a lifetime to achieve their goals, if they ever achieve them at all. Just in case anyone else has the same or a similar question, I have a little exercise that should answer the question as to whether or not we all need mentors or OPE, but it will also show you that you have always had them. Thus, the question really becomes, have you gotten the maximum effective use of such relationships? Take a look at the following chart:

	Super Bowl Champions	NBA Champions	World Series Champions		Teachers Names
2011				1st Grade	
2010				2nd Grade	
2009				3rd Grde	
2008				4th Grade	
2007				5th Grade	
2006				6th Grade	
2005				7th Grade	
2004				8th Grade	

I predict that many, if not a huge majority of you, can't recall the past champions in the major sports in America, but you will certainly recall the names of your past teachers. The reason why is quite obvious—you remember those who have an impact on your life. Most likely, that impact began with your parents, and then continued with your teachers. Les Brown, one my favorite motivational speakers, talks about a man named Mr. Washington, who had a major impact on his life by way of a simple, defining statement, "Someone else's opinion of you doesn't have to become your reality." Those simple words began a thought-changing process that has inspired and helped to change the lives of many—including mine!

If you are an entrepreneur or an aspiring entrepreneur, the most important thing for you to do at the start of your endeavor is to find someone who has had success doing what you want to do. When I first started in radio, I knew that I wanted to be just like my childhood hero. His name was Rick Party and I had grown up listening to him on WGCI, one of the biggest stations in Chicago. Rick had gone to work for a new station that was under a year old and was still in launch mode. Just as I was looking for a station to complete my internship, I learned that Rick was working at KISS 103.5 FM in Chicago, and they were in need of interns. I saw this as my opportunity to get next to the guy who, in my opinion, was the best in the business. I had to apply for a promotions internship, but Rick was a jock in the programming department. Still, I knew that all I had to do was get in the door and eventually I could meet Rick Party. In the interest of space, I'll spare you the details but know this: I met Rick Party and he became my mentor. The things that I learned from him took me much further than most of what I learned in school. Rick not only taught me about becoming a radio personality, but he also exposed me to another industry beyond radio—voiceovers. Because of Rick's advice, I was able to lock down my first commercial radio gig while many of my classmates never even broke into the industry. Most importantly, because of Rick's guidance, I was able to launch my first business. I am currently one of the voices that you hear day-to-day as the signature Radio Station Imaging voice, as well as concert and stage play promos and, of course, commercials. In fact, I just finished recording and producing a promo for the Broadway production of *DreamGirls* before I started typing this chapter. This would never have happened had I not had Rick Party as my mentor.

So how do you find a mentor? I'm glad you asked! The first thing to consider is who your hero is in your field. Whatever your field is, you want to learn from top-producing talent. Identify a person who has achieved honors and recognition within their company and industry over a period of time. Don't necessarily pick someone who is a "new guy" everyone is excited about—you need to learn from someone who has been tested and proven. Think of the years in a business like you would a life. A few months means this person isn't even walking yet! A person can only share their experience to the extent that they have lived; obviously, someone who has been in a field for ten years is better equipped to teach or mentor than someone with only one year's experience. Although there are some exceptions to this, I generally like to learn from more seasoned mentors. After you identify that person, you need to give them what I call the "WALLI" test. WALLI is an acronym for five key characteristics that I look for when choosing a mentor. By the way, that's the best part about the journey to success: unlike school, where your teachers were assigned to you for the most part, you choose who to learn from in life. So I use WALLI:

W – Willing to help me. It doesn't matter what someone knows if he or she is not willing to help me. If the candidate is not willing to help you, then they probably don't have much to offer anyway. I have never met a successful person who didn't want to help someone else. Earl Nightingale says, "Success is the progressive realization of a worthy ideal," so only losers are afraid to help others for fear of losing what they think they have.

A – Achieving New Goals. You should learn from people who are visionaries. They still have dreams and goals. If you learn from them, you also tend to develop their habits and this will keep you reaching for new goals, too. I call this idea "Forward Motion." Additionally, if you learn from someone with no vision, you will learn to have no vision as well, or, at best, you won't know what to do with your vision.

L – Loves What They Are Doing. When a person loves what they do, they bring a sense of excitement to the task. They are enthusiastic, which carries a creative and inspiring connotation. New ideas emerge and this leads to the greatest potential to attract good things.

L – Leadership. Simply put, a leader knows how to get things done. You want to become a great leader in your field. The best way to learn how to become a leader is to be mentored by one. Leaders also have access to other people, places, events and resources.

I – Integrity. Again this characteristic is paramount in a mentor. You want to work with someone who does what they say they will even if the feeling in which they said it in seems less than enthusiastic. That's commitment and honesty. People trust them and take their word; this will help you later.

Certainly, there are other characteristics that you can add to the list, but the "WALLI" test represents the key things that I believe make a good mentor. If the candidate passes the "WALLI" test, then you've got a mentor, but how do you get them to invest time in you? I say *invest*, because anyone who values their time only *spends* it with their family and close friends. With everyone else, they are *investing* time. With any investment, the investor is looking for a return on their investment (ROI), so what would that be in a mentor/mentee relationship? I was surprised to find that most successful people get satisfaction from helping others achieve their dreams and goals. Just knowing that they are giving birth to new life in many cases is ROI enough. Some like the idea of being able to say they had a hand in your success. Again, I have never met a selfish person who is successful but I'm sure they exist. I believe that this is because successful people realize that they didn't accomplish their goals on their own. Everyone who has ever achieved any worthy goal learned something of substantive value from someone else. Always remember that you don't need to re-create the wheel; the course has already been charted. All you need is the recipe that others have already used to prepare that fine cuisine we call success!

I always say, "Success is not a destination but a journey." After you reach your goal, new goals should be on the horizon, so you never truly stop reaching for success. When you find a good mentor, he or she will help you cut your learning curve and reduce the amount of time spent doing it. It would've taken me years to learn on my own what Rick Party taught me in days. Another major benefit of having a mentor is, many times, you simply don't know all the possibilities at your fingertips. A mentor who's been where you are can see things you can't yet. Rick Party showed me many possibilities; from there, I did the work necessary to maximize my potential. Once you have a mentor, hopefully you're inspired to do the same!

Earlier in the chapter I stated that, "Whether a mentor is necessary is not the question, but rather whether you gotten the maximum effective use of such relationships." We all know how to get answers to our questions from our mentors, but if that is all we are doing, then we are leaving a wealth of resources on the table. If your mentor is a respected leader in his or her field, then they will be attending events and sometimes hosting or facilitating events. This is where you become "Server in Chief!" No one should out-serve you. Anytime your mentor is speaking at a workshop, seminar or training event; you should be there. Volunteer to help set up and/or tear down equipment, sweep the floor, and carry their stuff. Whatever you have to do to be in that environment, as long as it's legal, DO IT! This commitment will show your mentor that you are serious about learning and being involved with whatever is happening in your field. You will learn more by watching your mentor in action as well. Most importantly, you will start gaining recognition from your mentor's peers. When you start to tap into your mentor's network, you are gaining something more valuable than money. Robert Kiyosaki, author of *Rich Dad, Poor Dad*, says, "You can tell a person's net worth by their network." Studies have shown that people generally earn the average of their closest five friends. So, if you want to earn more, you may need to upgrade your relationships.

I'm not saying you should choose your friends based on their income, but I am saying that you should have friends who are where you want to be. If you want to make great money, start serving your mentor and you will gain more than you can imagine. Most golden nuggets of knowledge get passed along, not on stages, but in the car or over coffee or dinner.

Your mentor can also be a great marketing tool. This is why you need to choose someone with integrity. People listen to people with a good reputation. As you prove yourself, your mentor will talk about you to other people. They may even use their reputation to help promote you. When you can get an endorsement from your mentor, it goes a long way and carries a lot of weight. Take pictures with your mentor, especially if he or she has a high profile or is a public figure. Let's face it; we live in a superficial world. If your mentor is a bestselling author or well-known person with people power and you are in many pictures with them and many of their peers, people are going to start to assume that you are one of them. I'm not saying you should act like something you are not, but, as Les Brown, my favorite motivational speaker, says, "Act how you want to be and pretty soon you'll be how you act." Finally, if you see an area that your mentor may benefit from something you do well, offer it as a way to help them. He or she will love you for it and tell their peers; pretty soon, everybody will be talking about the "new kid on the block" helping the old-school pros raise their game.

At the end of the day, you want to develop a genuine relationship with this person. She or he can and should be a lifelong mentor. Rick Party is still my mentor and I'm still chasing his accomplishments as my mentees are chasing mine! Every now and then, call your mentor, just to say hello. Not looking for an answer to an issue, not asking for anything—just calling to say hello. Offer to treat for lunch on occasion; people are really willing to help you when they know you are a person with a good heart. Then when you do need to ask for their help, they will not hesitate to be there for you.

If you see them working on something, offer to help. One of my mentors, Dr. John R. Porter, is the reason why I am a writer today. Dr. Porter is a pastor emeritus and former civil rights leader; in fact, I have a picture of him with Dr. Martin L. King Jr. in Chicago from the sixties. In 2007, Dr. Porter was writing a book named *The Autobiography of Black Male Violence*. I saw an opportunity to learn in the process of helping. My vernacular expanded, my social consciousness was awakened, and I learned how to write a book—all from helping Dr. Porter. He told me I had a brilliant mind and plenty of potential to be great, but I needed to develop a macro-perspective worldview. Dr. Porter was right—I soon learned that my views on the world were narrow and reflected a micro-perspective worldview. Once again, I didn't know everything I thought I knew—I didn't even know what I didn't know!"

This leads me to my final point: always remain coachable. There is nothing more irritating than dealing with someone who thinks they know something that they don't. We all should have a level of confidence about ourselves and our work. That confidence, however, has to be monitored periodically to make sure ego isn't developing. Confidence is healthy; ego is pride puffing itself up with the delirium of self-absorption. Nobody wants to help an egomaniac even if he or she is brilliant. I am always careful not to allow people's praise to go to my head. I know that I am good at what I do, but I always challenge myself to be better; this keeps me reasonably humble–humble enough to learn from anyone ready and willing to teach. So, if your mentor tells you that you need to do something, don't just blow them off because it doesn't make sense to you now, because their insight could mean the difference between failure and success. More importantly, it could be a test—if you fail that test, you may not get a chance to retake it for awhile, if ever.

A wise man once told me, "A man who knows something knows he knows nothing at all." This is my attitude as I approach learning. I am a sponge, here to soak up all the knowledge I can possibly absorb. This will be a healthy approach for you to take as well. I'll leave you with this thought: Mentors are something we have always had; the question is, have you gotten the maximum effective use from those relationships?

Angela Parkman-Wiggins is a licensed Certified Public Accountant and received her certification over 25 years ago from the state of Illinois. She enjoys using her knowledge and expertise to help business owners as well as individuals keep up with the demanding requirements of financial and tax reporting. She provides accounting, tax and advisory services to a wide variety of clientele. Angela is proficient in electronic filing tax returns and expediting tax refunds. She is also skilled in guiding new businesses thru the beginning stages of operation.

Currently, Angela holds the position of Senior Manager with the team of Brooks & Robertson, LLP, Certified Public Accountants. There she focuses her attention on clients in need of assistance with complex tax matters. Prior to joining Brooks & Robertson, LLP,

She brought thirteen years of experience as a Sole Proprietor with her to the partnership. Angela has always worked in the financial industry beginning with several years of service in banking. A strong desire to help others understand how to use the tax laws to their advantage has allowed Angela to express her passion for teaching. She often presents educational seminars on various tax related subjects. Angela currently serves on the board of directors for the South Suburban Small Business Association as a board member for more than ten years with nearly eight of those years holding the position as Treasurer. She also held the position as Chief Financial Officer for a nonprofit social service agency for over five years.

Contact Information:
Email: mytaxangel@gmail.com
Phone: (708) 432-6018

Chapter 16

Managing Your Money Wisely

Angela Wiggins

How does an Unstoppable Entrepreneur manage his or her money? It's very simple. When you know better, you do better. What I mean by that is when you know what the results are expected to be, you have more control over the process.

For example: You decide to buy a brand new piece of equipment for your business because you believe that it will increase your productivity and result in increased profits. Your goal is to make more money. You find out how much the equipment will cost, and then you evaluate all of your options for ways to pay for that equipment. You'll choose the option(s) that will help you get that equipment in the shortest amount of time while costing you the least amount of your own resources. Your most valuable resources are your time and your money. So you create a plan. Your plan will take into account all of variables that you are aware of at that time. Variables such as: how much money will I need? How much money do I have? How much money can I raise? Where will I get the money? How long will it take me to raise the money? How much money can I expect to make from this equipment? And after you have honestly answered all of those questions, then and only then will you be able to answer the most important question of them all: *Is it worth all the effort?*

If you find satisfactory answers to all of your questions, you can feel pretty confident that your outcome will be very close to your expectations. This level of confidence comes only with having a plan and following it.

There are six simple steps for a successful entrepreneur to manage his or her money wisely. Although I will be discussing how to manage your business finances here, the same rules will also apply to your personal financial activities.

I am a Certified Public Accountant. I like to see things laid out in a logical order because I think that order makes things easier to understand. If my instructions are easy to understand, then I am more likely to follow them as directed. If I follow them as directed and find success, then repeating the steps also becomes easier. If I repeat the steps over and over again, then I will create a new habit. I would say that managing your money wisely is a very good habit to have. Wouldn't you agree?

So here are the six simple steps that will help you to manage your money wisely.
1. Create a plan
2. Write it down
3. Follow the plan
4. Evaluate the results
5. Make any necessary adjustments
6. Repeat the process

Although the steps are simple, many don't follow them. Many skip some or all of the steps and hit the ground running. But an Unstoppable Entrepreneur follows each step exactly as directed because they know that having a plan and following that plan is what makes them truly UNSTOPPABLE.

1. <u>YOU MUST HAVE A PLAN</u>

As it is with anything that you want to do successfully, you must have a plan. The same is true when managing your money. Without a plan, it can be easy to lose focus of your goal. Usually a plan starts with an idea. That idea may be sparked by a problem that you can see that needs a solution. You may begin to ask yourself questions such as, "What can be done to solve that problem?" or, "How can I fix that problem?" As you think about your questions, your mind will begin to search for solutions to the problem.

For example, you visit a coffee shop every now and then. And almost every time you go there, they mix up your order and then have to re-make it. Now you continue to visit the shop because your visits are irregular and you believe that they will eventually get the problem resolved. But you notice that 9 out of 10 visits result in yet another mix up. You have already spoken to the manager on more than one occasion about the recurring problem, so you begin to ask yourself questions such as, "I wonder how many other customers are having this same problem?" Then, the entrepreneur in you begins to see a problem that needs a solution. And this problem could lead you to a business opportunity. So you begin to study the problem and you may come up with an idea that can solve the problem. That idea turns into a mental picture and you may even begin to see a way to solve that problem. You might even see a way to make some money while doing it. After all, isn't that exactly what an entrepreneur does? Find an opportunity and turn it into a profitable business? SBA.gov defines an entrepreneur as *"A person who sees an opportunity, makes a plan, starts the business, manages the business and receives the profits."*

Creating your plan should help you find the answers to questions such as, "How much does it cost to run a coffee shop?" or, "What kind of profits can I expect from operating a shop like this?" or, "What do I need to do to make this shop more successful than it is already?" and, "Who is my competition?"

Your plan should also serve as your financial road map that shows where **you** want to go. It should let you know if you are on the right path or lost in the woods. Not only is it a guide, it will help you determine how much money you'll need to complete your journey. After all, you would never go on the trip of your dreams and then find out that you did not have enough money to get back home, would you?

Your financial road map can also be referred to as a budget. A budget is really a financial projection that tells a story about your idea. It tells how much money you think you'll need to successfully reach your goal while taking into account all information available to you at the time. It will also lay out how much money you expect to make while on the road to your goal. Your budget should cause you to ask yourself questions such as, "How much will this whole thing cost?" and "Where will the funds come from?" These are undoubtedly tough questions, but every Unstoppable Entrepreneur will need to know the answers to them at some point in their process.

Having well thought out answers to these questions gives you more control over the results of your efforts. Not only does your plan give you more control, it also keeps you focused on what you are trying to accomplish. With that kind of focused control, there is no doubt that you will be Unstoppable.

Your numbers tell a story. And if the story is clear and well thought out, then others will be able to see your plan almost as clearly as you can. When that happens, you'll find it easier to secure the funds needed to complete your project. However, if your numbers tell a story that is not well thought out, you may find it extremely difficult to secure outside funding.

2. <u>YOUR PLAN MUST BE IN WRITING</u>

Your written financial plan makes your idea crystal clear so that others can see what your mind sees. It is also a guide for you to follow. It will lead you to where you want to go with the least amount of time, energy, and usually by the shortest distance. In the example of the coffee shop, your goal would be to turn an average coffee shop into a more profitable business venture; a coffee shop that would have a much higher level of customer satisfaction, resulting in a larger customer base. Your goal is to turn the occasional customer into a regular customer.

As you go about formalizing your idea(s) into a financial plan, you must write it down. If your plan is not written, you will find yourself telling the same story over and over again. In addition, you will probably find it difficult to explain your numbers in an easy to understand manor. Your written plan serves several purposes:

a) First, it tells the story of your idea(s) in dollars and cents. No one can tell your story as well as you can. It shows how much or how little thought you have put into your plan. It is an excellent tool to help others see a clear and detailed picture of how your plan will come to life. Your story does not have to be the final edition. It can and should be revised as needed.

b) Your written plan serves as your road map. It should guide you to your chosen destination. It helps to keep you from being easily distracted by unrelated sights, sounds and ideas. There will always be someone or something pulling at you for your time, attention and your money. It can be very easy to be lead off your chosen course and not even realize it. But having a written plan and referring to it often can assist you in making decisions that will help you reach your goal so much faster. After all, why would you want to take the long way home when you know the short cut?

c) Your written plan helps to keep you focused on your goal so that you will use your resources more wisely and not get side tracked.

d) It also allows you see any weaknesses or obstacles in your plan. You'll need to identify them and determine how you will handle them before they arise. It may even help you to avoid some of them all together. Although, not all plans will go exactly as desired, with some thought, you may even be able to turn a weakness into an advantage.

e) The process of creating your financial plan and writing it down will show early on in the process whether your idea makes good financial sense or not. Is it a win-win proposition for everyone involved? After all, you wouldn't want to invest a significant amount time and money only to find that your idea did not produce your desired results. All too often, new entrepreneurs find that their project stalls due to lack of funds. It happens all the time to those who don't have a written plan. But the writing process will help to remove most of the uncertainty. When that happens, you begin to feel unstoppable.

f) If your plan is a really good one and your financial projection shows that your idea is a profitable one, you should have very few problems raising the funds needed to complete the project. Why? Because those who are in a position to help you financially will be able to see (in black & white) that your plan is a good one. They'll see that you have already thought about every possible problem and have already planned for a solution. A well thought out business plan along with a well thought out financial plan will attract the funding you will need. But only if it is written so that potential investors and/or lenders can read and understand your thoughts. Remember, your numbers tell a story.

g) Your written plan will allow you to measure your progress. You can evaluate how you are really doing on your journey compared to how you thought you would be doing. You will be able to measure whether you are on track and racing toward your goal, off track and sight-seeing, spinning your wheels and stuck in the mud, or falling behind and taking a nap.

3. <u>YOU MUST FOLLOW YOUR PLAN</u>
The next thing to do is to follow your plan. That's right. Test it out. See if it works the way you thought it would. Refer to it as often as necessary to check the status of your progress. Don't make a move until you have consulted the road map that you created. Check to see where you are today compared to where you were yesterday. Check to see if where you are today is where you thought you would be today. Are you ahead of schedule, behind schedule or right on target?

Are you still on the right path or have you drifted off your chosen path for some sight-seeing? Is your plan working as you thought it would or does it need to be revised?

Is your plan revealing things that you did not think of? If so, how will those things affect your outcome (reaching your goal)? Do you need to make changes to your plan? Or has your plan revealed that your idea is not such a good idea after all? Discovering that your idea is not as good as you thought it would be is so much better if found out earlier rather than later.

This discovery can save you a lot of time, energy and of course money. If you follow your plan, your chances for success will increase exponentially. After all, what good is it to have a plan and not follow it? That would be like throwing your road map out the window.

4. **YOU MUST EVALUATE YOUR RESULTS**
   How is your plan working? Are you on track? Are you getting the results that you thought you would get? Is your plan revealing strengths or weakness that you weren't aware of or maybe had not thought of? How can you use this information to your advantage? Do you need to make changes or scrap the whole plan and start over? Have your goals changed? These are all tough questions but they are designed to get you to your desired goal with the least amount of your own resources.

Regularly evaluating your results will help you identify most flaws and weaknesses in your plan before someone else does, thereby allowing you the opportunity to make adjustments and improvements that will strengthen your plan. Continuous evaluations will allow you to be able to answer most questions and/or objections that may come your way. In addition, evaluating your results will highlight your strengths that can be used to promote the value of your plan.

You must test the validity of your plan by actually following it step by step. That way, you will know if it really works the way you thought it would. After all, it is **your** plan. Just keep in mind that the numbers always tell a story and you need to know exactly what your numbers are saying.

5. ADJUST YOUR PLAN OF ACTION AS NECESSARY

Referring often to your written plan allows you to evaluate your progress and make any necessary adjustments or corrections to your actions. It should be designed to help you stay on track. But most of all, it should let you know if your plan makes good business sense. You will only be able to make adjustments to your plan if you have followed the steps. If you have not completed the first four steps, how will you know if you are on track? How will you know how close you really are to obtaining your goal? If you have completed the first four steps and have evaluated your progress, you can now see what adjustments (if any) you need to make. You'll be able to

see if your idea is still a good idea and if it makes sense. And if it is still a good idea, you will be able to visualize your plan even clearer than you did before. As your plan grows clearer and stronger, it becomes more impossible for anyone or anything to get in your way.

Look at the example business budget on the following page. It shows a financial example of what the business owner thought would happen verses what actually did happen. As he began to analyze the variances, he made some notes to explain them. For example, his note next to utilities was "Too high." Now he may focus his attention on ways to reduce his utilities cost.

A variety of budget forecasting templates can be found at **www.Office.Microsoft.com**, or **www.Score.org/templates**.

6. **REPEAT THE PROCESS**

If you have followed all of the previous steps and found success, your next step should be to do it over and over again. You should use this process on everything that is important to you. Any dreams and/or desires that you may have can be obtained by following these six steps. Once you have turned this process into a habit, you will have earned the title of the UNSTOPPABLE ENTREPRENEUR.

Remember, you are an entrepreneur. You find the opportunities. You create the plans. You put the plans into action. You manage the actions. And you reap the rewards. That is what makes you an UNSTOPPABLE ENTREPRENEUR.

BUSINESS BUDGET

Month/Year: Aug-12

SUMMARY	ACTUAL	BUDGETED	OVER BUDGET	UNDER BUDGET
Total income	1,432,500.00	1,318,080.00	114,420.00	
Total expenses	339,760.00	314,910.00	24,850.00	
Income less expenses:	1,092,740.00	1,003,170.00	89,570.00	

INCOME DETAILS	ACTUAL	BUDGETED	OVER BUDGET	UNDER BUDGET	NOTES
Sales	1,400,000.00	1,200,000.00	200,000.00		Increase advertising next year.
Interest earned	5,000.00	4,500.00	500.00		
Fees	1,000.00	980.00	20.00		
Commissions	10,000.00	98,000.00		(88,000.00)	
Rent	9,000.00	8,000.00	1,000.00		
Royalties	2,500.00	2,600.00		(100.00)	
Other	5,000.00	4,000.00	1,000.00		
Total income:	1,432,500.00	1,318,080.00	114,420.00		

EXPENSE DETAILS	ACTUAL	BUDGETED	OVER BUDGET	UNDER BUDGET	NOTES
SELLING					
Salaries and wages	246,000.00	248,000.00		(2,000.00)	
Commissions	10,000.00	12,000.00		(2,000.00)	
Advertising	6,000.00	8,000.00		(2,000.00)	Increase Here 3%.
Travel	4,600.00	5,600.00		(1,000.00)	
Other	1,000.00	1,200.00		(200.00)	
Total sales expenses:	267,600.00	274,800.00		(7,200.00)	
Percent of total:	78.76%	87.26%			
ADMINISTRATIVE					
Salaries and wages	12,000.00	10,000.00	2,000.00		
Employee benefits	5,000.00	6,000.00		(1,000.00)	
Payroll taxes	500.00	500.00			
Insurance	14,000.00	14,000.00			
Loans	6,000.00	5,000.00	1,000.00		
Office supplies	4,000.00	4,100.00		(100.00)	
Travel & entertainment	200.00	190.00	10.00		
Postage	300.00	320.00		(20.00)	
Total admin. expenses:	42,000.00	40,110.00	1,890.00		
Percent of total:	12.36%	12.74%			
SERVICE & EQUIPMENT					
Accounting	1,200.00	1,500.00		(300.00)	
Legal	5,000.00	6,000.00		(1,000.00)	
Utilities	15,000.00	15,789.00		(789.00)	Too high.
Telephone	5,000.00	4,800.00	200.00		
Equipment purchases	3,400.00	3,000.00	400.00		
Rent & maintenance	560.00	600.00		(40.00)	
Total S&E expenses:	30,160.00	31,689.00		(1,529.00)	
Percent of total:	8.88%	10.06%			

Microsoft Office Template

Da-Nay "The Conquering Coach" Macklin is a Mother, Wife, Entrepreneur, Author, Speaker, Certified Life Coach and Career Consultant. She specializes in life purpose, transformational, and adultery coaching providing her clients the luxury of being able to live life by design rather than default. She has been featured on ABC-7, My 50 Chicago, and WYCA and a host of other media outlets.

Da-Nay earned her Bachelors Degree (BS) in Business Management from the University of Illinois at Chicago. She received her coaching training and Certified Christian Life Coach certification from the Professional Christian Coaching and Counseling Academy. She is also a member of Coach Training Alliance. Additional coach training includes: Comprehensive Coaching U, Incorporated, and The Coaching Institute.

Da-Nay is the President and Founder of Da-Nay Macklin Inc., where she is dedicated and passionate in assisting clients to design individualized lifestyles based on their passion and purpose. *She takes her clients from broken to breakthroughs!*

Da-Nay is a published contributing author for The Unstoppable Woman's Guide to Emotional Well-Being. She has held and holds many leadership positions along with memberships including the National Association of Professional Women. She is also a contributor to numerous publications and her proprietary monthly newsletter, "Confront & Conquer." Da-Nay has spoken at numerous seminars, conferences and workshops focusing on empowering and encouraging audiences across the country and was featured on the BOSS Network's "Behind the Business: A Real Look at Women in Leadership."

Da-Nay is a keynote speaker as well as a trainer. Audiences love her transparency, contagious charisma, and genuine nature. She welcomes you and thanks you in advance for visiting her at:
www.danaymacklin.com
www.facebook.com/theconqueringcoach
Call: 1-888-656-9970 or E-Mail: **danay@danaymacklin.com**

Chapter 17

Weaning the Workaholic

Da-Nay Macklin

All business owners dread burnout, and entrepreneurs even more so because the additional risks they have taken constantly nag their minds, creating a fear of failure that can push them to that point.

According to *Psychology Today*, burnout occurs:
1. When you are not in control of how you carry out your job
2. When you are working toward goals that do not resonate with you
3. When you lack social support
4. When you don't tailor your responsibilities to your true calling
5. When you don't take a break once in a while

A two-year study of 2,235 participants discovered that conflicts between work and home time vying for priority in year one, predicted burnout in year two.

You know you have burnout when you have given all of yourself, your time and effort. You are exhausted and more than a little cynical, and you absolutely have no energy or ideas left to give. Sound familiar? If so, you are not alone! Ultimately this is a place you never want to be.

As an entrepreneur, risk of burnout is high, so it is critical to protect yourself by being aware of what you are doing and how you are feeling. There are several factors to consider when preventing burnout:

1. **To prevent burnout, you need a social support system**:

The most common cause of burnout is being stretched too thin. For a woman entrepreneur, especially if you have a family, burnout can be a deal-breaker. Ideally, you can rely on other adults (your husband, friends, parents...) who are excited for you and who will pitch in with the children and home responsibilities while you set up your new or existing business. If you are forced to go it alone, at some point you may become too drained from being both mom and entrepreneur, suffer burnout, and ultimately have to give up your dream. However, I'm pleading for you to NEVER give up on any of YOUR dreams! You are not a quitter, are you? Exactly! The way to prevent burnout is to structure home responsibilities. This often means bringing in a home support team. You may also need a work support team. Most people can go for a period of time with very little sleep, lots of stress, too much caffeine (I plead the fifth)☺, and not coming up for air as they work towards setting up their dream business. At some point, however, they <u>will</u> have to get sleep, tone down the stress, skip the coffee, and take a deep breath. It's when they believe they are Superman or Superwoman and continue to abuse their bodies to reach that next objective, that they become at risk for burnout. Before you reach the point where you can't go on, activate your common sense. If you have too much to do and too little time to do it, get an assistant. If you don't have money yet to hire anyone, bring in an intern or a volunteer. Personally I love and swear by www.internships.com. Here you will find quality interns saving you time and money. The Superman and Superwoman syndrome tries to convince us that we can do it all by ourselves. Don't believe the hype! Bring people in to work with you. Getting fresh eyes on the problem will generate creative ideas and ward off burnout.

2. To prevent burnout, take a break once in a while:

A second cause of burnout is the mistaken belief that whenever you are alone, that is "Me" time. We all need private or "Me" time.

This is our opportunity to slow down, relax and regroup. Our brains get overloaded from too much input. We've had to make too many decisions, and our emotions get tangled up. We are exhausted and need to do something else, so that our brain has a chance to sort through it all. Too often women entrepreneurs assume that working alone on the business counts as "Me" time. Yes, we are alone doing what we love and are committed to, but this is not giving our minds and bodies the break they need. After intensive work, we need to press the "reset button." An athlete has to take a breather after 50 reps of an exercise to allow his muscles to get rid of the lactic acid that builds up in them during repeated contractions. Once he gives his muscles a break, he can do another 50 reps. Our brains are no different. When we feel that we need a break, we usually really need it. If we repeatedly push through and ignore our body's warning signals of fatigue, we will end up with burnout.

3. To prevent burnout, take control of your work.

The third cause of burnout is allowing stresses from our personal life to interfere with work. We entrepreneurs assume that since we chose to set up our own business, that we are totally focused on our work. Yet, often, without realizing it, we bring our personal lives to work with us. People who are able to compartmentalize usually avoid mixing work and non-work. Men seem to do this instinctively. Actually, according to studies, most men easily isolate different aspects of their lives, such work versus home, emotions verses logic, while women tend to integrate them. Why should that matter? When we are with family and friends, we all develop emotional connections that tie our various activities with them together. These bonds are healthy and beneficial. On the other hand, in work settings, this same emotional connection with our personal life can be a serious hindrance. Whatever our work responsibilities, anything related to our personal lives needs to be set aside in order for us to perform our jobs efficiently and effectively. Unfortunately, for the most part, women find this hard to do.

Women can easily juggle five or six simultaneous projects related to caring for spouses, children, home, friends and hobbies. Because this kind of multitasking requires that our emotions constantly interact with our activities, it seems to come naturally, and we do quite well with this.

In the entrepreneurial world, however, we discover that we have to block out our personal life at least to some degree in order to perform work tasks well. Even in a standard business setting, if we allow thoughts and emotions unrelated to our work to backwash onto our jobs, our efficiency level drops drastically from the distraction and our energy is quickly sapped from being pulled in diverse directions.

Here is where compartmentalizing comes in handy. For most men, this is a "no brainer": just separate your home life from work responsibilities. Seems simple enough, but due to the structure of women's brains, this does not come naturally for us. We understand cognitively why it is necessary, but the *how* eludes us. Unfortunately, compartmentalizing is something we have to teach ourselves to do if we ever expect to be successful in business.

This backflow of thoughts and emotion from one part of our brain to the other is similar to what dyslexic children experience when they try to study. Non-dyslexic children utilize the left side of their brains more than the right side when learning a new concept. This is because the left hemisphere of the brain handles details, logic and sequencing, while the right hemisphere sees the "big picture" and plans out strategies. Dyslexic children instinctively try to grasp concepts by using both sides of the brain simultaneously, which prevents them from processing details in the correct order. Because their two hemispheres interact so seamless, they cannot prevent a backwash from one side to the other until they learn how and when to use each side effectively.

According to studies, adult women also experience a backwash of brain activity between hemispheres. Consequently, we bring our whole emotional life experience to the table for every decision. This sounds as though it would be an asset. Unfortunately, unless we consciously sort out which emotions and thoughts are pertinent at any one time, this emotional clutter will get in the way of our making quick, efficient, well-attuned decisions for a particular work task. Moreover, we will continually have to second-guess our decisions—and rightly so—because they were made while we were in the haze of conflicting thoughts as to the best solution.

As a woman entrepreneur, if we are unaware of how our brains function, we will be limited in our level of success and have no idea why. We will just keep driving ourselves more and more, but not making progress—almost like trying to run up a hill made of slippery mud. This frustration inevitably causes out-of-control stress, and eventually, burnout.

Please know I'm not saying you have to totally divest yourself of all emotion to be an effective entrepreneur. Operating like a robot at work would alienate both your staff and clients. You need to work WITH your brain instead of against it. Accept the fact that you have emotions. You would have never even considered becoming an entrepreneur unless you already had imagination, creativity, smarts and drive. Emotion is linked to every one of these qualities. As a dreamer, you have strong emotional ties to your cutting edge ideas. You feel a deep personal sense of accomplishment for everything you've achieved so far. You love the thrill of pushing yourself to the limit. You are an emotional being. Although it may not seem like it right now, these emotions are actually one of your strengths.

Being an entrepreneur, you have formulated a strategy to build your dream business. It involves critical steps that take your seed of an idea and grow it into a living, breathing entity that will change life for a lot of people. *In the same way, you can design a Compartmentalizing Strategy that will make you able to focus on work and prevent burnout.* It will help you evaluate yourself, your strengths and weaknesses—including how you think, react, and function. Here is how:

- Create a mental "on/off switch" that lets you shift gears from family to work in a split second. Train yourself to respond to visual, auditory and kinetic triggers that you have designed for yourself. For example: listen to an energetic or motivating CD on the way to work, recite positive statements like, "I'm going to make a positive difference today," or have a set morning routine once you sit at your desk. These are powerful triggers that enable you to push aside thoughts and emotions not related to your work.

- Organize your home life to prevent emotional stress from interfering with your workday. Create a checklist of your weekly family responsibilities. Make sure that everything is taken care of sufficiently by bedtime, so that the next morning you are not carrying additional worries to work with you. This includes arranging ahead of time for getting your children to and from school, sports practice, dance lessons, etc.

  Your ability to focus as an entrepreneur is crucial. Without this you lose your creative edge. Separating your home responsibilities, and the emotions linked with them, from work tasks enables you to concentrate fully.

- Organize your work environment to keep stress levels low. This means letting your entire staff know what is expected of them, clarifying deadlines, and motivating them to feel that they are part of a unique enterprise that will benefit them as well. A team that understands their part in the whole will support you all the way. They will be there to fill in the gaps so that you don't have to. When stress is minimal in your work environment, you will be the most productive.

- Make your emotions work FOR you. Obviously, the claim that women are too emotional to run a business is ridiculous. Don't get me started! ☺ Nevertheless, *emotions are something women have to deal with because of the way our brains handle them.* If you ignore how your emotions affect your decision-making, you will risk making unprofessional and/or impulsive choices. You could even jeopardize your entire business. Your staff and employees need to know that the decisions you make are well thought through and at the same time take into account their needs and the company's wellbeing. Unless you make your emotions work for you, you cannot achieve that dual goal.

To accomplish this, you need to separate the emotions you can use to enhance your business strategy from those that are not particularly helpful. Emotions provide you with power— not to manipulate, but to *motivate.* Your business-friendly emotions can range from caring for others, to getting excited about an innovative idea, to frustration over inefficiency. Jot down all of your emotions that are business friendly, then assign each to a specific part of your business venture. The more you are aware of your own emotions and of ways they can empower you and your team, the more effective you will be as an entrepreneur!

Both men and women risk "burnout" when they allow their personal life and the emotions linked to it to come with them to work. The struggle to maintain focus drains you until you have no energy to be an entrepreneur. By compartmentalizing and determining which of your emotions are business-friendly, you will empower yourself to be successful. Most of all remember and MAKE time to have FUN! While in corporate America, it was a no brainer to take a fun vacation…I was PAID for vacations! As an entrepreneur, I find myself non-stop like a train on a track with no brakes. Sure, I want a vacation, but find myself saying "who has time for a vacation?" Sound familiar?

We lose our focus and clarity, resulting in poor decision making. Our creativity gets interrupted and no juices are flowing. Fatigue sits in where five cups of coffee later and you still can't get in gear. For crying out loud take a break! Or explore the below for an "entrepreneur's vacation:"

1. Read a good book - anything that will let your imagination run free and the creativity flow.

2. Hang out in a coffee shop - you'll meet the most interesting people or just people watch.

3. Go for a drive – I will often jump in the car and just go!

4. Have lunch with a friend – your pick☺

5. Go to a mid-day matinee - be really adventurous and try something new.

6. Enjoy a hobby – swimming, gardening, skating whatever it is, give yourself some time to have fun with it.

7. Play games with friends – find your inner child again.

8. Get some culture - Visit a museum or two - be a tourist in your own town.

9. Spend the afternoon with a child - if you don't have any of your own, borrow mine (just-kidding) or a friend's child and do something you would never do unless you were a child!

10. Treat yourself to a spa day – oh yeah! It is something that is good for both sexes.

When my clients (www.danaymacklin.com) get stressed out and can't figure "it" out, I give them an assignment to take time off and reflect while enjoying life again. The pay off for taking breaks can be monumentally amazing! Have you found yourself reading the same sentence over and over again? Or when you sit staring at the computer for over 15 minutes, trying to remember what you were just working on, it's time to take a break! Have fun with life and just enjoy YOU for a few hours. Trust that nothing awful will happen and you will be much more productive and successful as an Entrepreneur. Lastly, please do your Coach Da-Nay a big favor and try not to take too many "entrepreneurs vacations." ☺

Ogor Winnie Okoye is the consummate "Happy" multi-tasker! She is the author of "Awaken and Unleash Your Victor; Uncover the path to your magnificent Destiny", a motivational and inspiring guide to living a fearless, happy and successful life. She is an avid writer and blogger who has published a lot of articles on the topic of love, relationships and positive living. Ogor is an attorney by profession and the founder of BOS Legal, LLC, an immigration and criminal defense law firm located in Lynn, Massachusetts, U.S.A.

She is a mother to four beautiful children, and married to Dr. Victor Ide-Okoye, whom she readily describes as the wind beneath her wings!

Ogor started her legal career at the other far end of the globe in Nigeria, where she obtained a Bachelor's in law from the University of Nigeria, Enugu Campus in 1998. She went on to obtain a Juris Doctorate in law from the Suffolk University Law School in Boston, Massachusetts in 2003. She has been a trial Attorney in the Commonwealth of Massachusetts ever since. Ogor is an ardent champion and believer in LOVE as the most powerful and positive force of all, capable of healing and eradicating every conceivable problem in the world today. She believes that LOVE and the application of the Golden Rule should be the primary guiding principle in every human endeavor hence her insistence that her law practice be fully aligned with the application of both. She has had thousands of happy clients whose lives have been changed for the better as a result of this practice! As far as Ogor is concerned, lasting success in both personal and business relationships can only come from a place that imbibes and practices these twin virtues.

Chapter 18

Golden Rules for a Golden Business

Ogor Winnie Okoye

In today's competitive business world, the demand and desire to build a golden business trumps every other consideration. Every business owner would do whatever is needed to achieve short and long term success in their business. A thorough understanding and application of the tenets of the Golden rule can be instrumental in establishing and growing a solid and sound business. Most people believe that this rule only applies in interpersonal relationships between people and have not taken the additional step of extending the same tenet of the Golden Rule to their businesses.

The golden rule is as old as man and its simplest dictate is, "Do unto others as you would have them do unto you." Simple you might think, right? Yet, extremely difficult for most people and businesses to apply! The few people who understand that the fundamental human longing, be it in a private, personal relationship or a business relationship is the need to be validated and to feel appreciated and respected; and who go a step further in applying this simple time-tested dictate will do a lot better than most other businesses.

Customers have been known to travel long distances to a particular business simply because they received great customer service from that business. In a time like this marked by challenging economic times, every business needs to be on its toes in order to command a healthy and vibrant customer base.

Businesses need to train its employees, especially the front-line employees that interact with customers that they must embrace and cultivate the habit of being pleasant even if their private life is ridden with immense crisis. An atmosphere that is accommodating, friendly, and pleasant is an instant magnet for great business and believe it or not, even good fortune! A stressful or hostile environment is palpable and can be felt by any customer who walks in. I remember taking my daughter to a dance studio in the small town where we live and being instantly repelled by the owner's energy and demeanor. I instantly felt unwelcomed and was quite surprised when my daughter pulled me aside and said, "It seems people are not nice around here." Here is a then 8 year old telling me precisely what I felt but could not mouth because I did not want to dampen the excitement we felt before stepping into that ice-cold dance studio. I thought it was smart to reserve my comment for later in case it was me who was being hyper-sensitive and was erroneously imagining that the owner's demeanor was totally hostile. Two years later, I was talking to another parent whose child also danced at another dance studio about her experience with her current dance studio. She was gushing about how wonderful, nice and friendly they were over there, unlike a certain place she had taken her daughter to where the owner's hostile and foul demeanor made her vow she would never go back even if that was the only dance studio left in the world. To my utter surprise, she was talking about the same place that my daughter and I felt the acidic demeanor of the proprietor of the studio! Same place!! Unbeknownst to this business, they had been repelling and self-sabotaging their business for the longest time and were not even aware of this. Needless to say that this is no way to build a golden business.

Every customer who walks into a business has to feel that sense of welcome and warmth in the air. That is so very pivotal to the success of any business. There may be a huge competition for a particular brand of service or product, and so the business that makes its distinction in the way that it treats it customers usually is the one that will thrive and soar in spite of the fierce competition, which eventually translates to a robust bottom-line.

What is Your Brand?

In order to build a golden business you must, amongst other things, build a unique and rock-solid brand. Building a brand encompasses three key elements:

- Super customer service
- Well trained employees
- A well-organized company firmly grounded on ethical considerations

Branding controls virtually every action in the venture with each point of customer contact. A well-articulated mission controls employees and customers to think and perceive a company in terms of constructive brand qualities such as good quality, dependability, trust, and reliability.

A well organized and carefully articulated business plan remains pivotal to its long and short term success. Condition-sine qua non! When I talk about a well-organized business plan, I mean the company's products, web sites, corporate social responsibility (CSR), publications, phone etiquette, and the list goes on and on. Without a well-defined strategy and clearly stated business plan or mission statement, small or large business's efforts can be the case of unanticipated disaster after another. Difficult questions must be asked and answered by every serious business owner who truly desires to reach record growth and success, especially in this extremely competitive global economy.

Consumers want more than one variety and one size no longer fits all. If you look at the most successful business people and organizations, you will always see they display specific, unique, and sometimes discrete traits.

It is easy to know if you have built a golden business; you can tell this when your organization can endure and flourish in the competitive market by constantly responding to the changes of opportunities and threats. The performance of an organization is a key sign used to assess its competitive advantage. Organizations that recognize their customers and competitors in the market can expand new products that can deliver superior profit to their customers, and cost advantages over their competitors.

Building "The" Ethical Business

The impetus for building an ethical business in this competitive business world has never been more compelling. That is a huge part of the Golden rule! "Do unto others as you would have them do to you" The tenets of this rule demands that you as a business owner place yourself in the role of the customer to genuinely understand what it means to have a magnificent experience. As we know, both employees and customers are the most important stakeholders of any business. These two groups of people cannot be separated from any business, and they all must complement each other, otherwise the business cannot stand. In growing my own small business, I have found the golden rule to be instrumental to the growth and success of my firm and continually advocate the same for every small and large business owners.

The role of Corporate Social Responsibility in Organizations

When business has a good corporate social responsibility, it means essentially that they are ethically sound. They understand the tenets of the Golden Rule and have programs specifically targeted to help their employees, customer and the communities where they operate. Treating their employees fairly, providing a good working environment, and paying them fairly and appropriately are very useful in the long and short term growth of any company irrespective of its size. Employees perform better when they sense that their employer is treating them as justly as possible.

Superb Customer Service
A company's life-line is its customers and without them, no business can survive. Therefore, a huge onus lies on the smart business owner to do everything and anything possible to keep its customers coming back while also attracting new ones. When they are satisfied, they will come back, and if they come back your business will prosper. A satisfied customer is a repeat customer and in most cases they will bring their friends and family, thereby growing your business; that, makes a business golden.

Making your business environment customer-friendly is part of the customer service equation. Customers would return time and time again to a business that is not necessarily close to them, but to one that they feel treated them with the utmost sense of respect and civility. Proximity is never a problem when a customer enjoyed unique services those other similarly-situated businesses were unable to offer them. Something as simple as offering customers a coffee station where they can brew and drink coffee in the morning with bagels and muffins provided free of charge may be an incentive for the customer to pass other similar businesses and drive a longer distance just to get to that customer-friendly business.

A seating area with warm welcoming colors and comfortable seats, magazines, television, makes customers feel relaxed in place of business and when you happen to have one of those hectic days and a customer had to wait before being attended to, that long period of waiting would fly by in an instant in an environment where the customer feels relaxed and entertained.

Creating a Solid and Well Trained Employee Base

It is a truism that employees are more productive when their inputs are encouraged and accepted by their firms. Today's workforce prefers to work for firms who share their core value. They also want to work for firms with an outstanding CSR programs that take care of its employees, communities and society in general. In today's market, employees want more than their weekly paycheck, they want to be part of the decision-making process in their firms, and they want that to reflect in their employment contract. Employees feel comfortable working for firms that they can trust to give them the opportunities to contribute their opinions to their immediate business environment. They are ready to find those firms no matter where and how. Companies are responding to the demand of today's employees and they are adjusting their business policies to accommodate these employees.

In a smaller business environment, a successful business owner would understand and appreciate the role others play in the advancement of his or her business, and so would always be in parallel roles with the other person in whatever capacity he/she operates. They must become what I often refer to as "a certified role-switcher." In order words, the gnawing question in their mind at any given time is, "What would I demand from this business as an employee even though I am the owner?" Answers to questions such as these gives some clarity and insight into the key ingredients required for creating a solid and happy employee base. Questions such as these make the business think in terms of the much broader role of advancing the long-term goals of the organization.

Essentially, it is the employees who are responsible for the day to day management of the business and if their needs are met, they are better able to advance both the long-term and short-term goals of the business. Employees form the back-bone of any business and they are the ones that interact most with customers and vendors. The effect of the most pleasant, kind, friendly or great employer or business owner is hardly felt by the customers but can be felt if and only if the employer is able to galvanize the same positive energy and vibration into his employees. When employees understand that the owner of the business has their best interests at heart, they are working harder and smarter for the organization. Their positive energy and earnest effort trickles down to the customers and keep them coming back time and time again.

The bottom line is that employees are one of a firm's best assets as they are among the top shareholders of the firms and should be treated as such. As one of the top shareholders of the firms, employees should be part of the decision-making process in the business. Employers should allow and encourage their employees to help their firms reach their long and short term goals as reflected in their mission statement. Firms should help their employees stick to the firms' vision consistent with its strategic business direction.

Customers gauge the mood of the employees working in a business and often times would judge the business based on the nature of treatment that they received from those employees. Employees who go over and above the call of duty and who inject a level of joy, passion and dedication to their jobs always attract more and more customers to a business than the employees who are aloof, hostile or simply unfriendly. You are a billboard for your business; you are your brand!

What most small and medium sized businesses fail to recognize is the fact that they are walking billboards for their organizations. If an organization purports to be into health and wellness and the owner or top executives of the organization are battling with being overweight, it is a no brainer that it will be an uphill task for that business to soar to its desired expectation. In the same vein, if a business purports to be welcoming and understanding and then choose to recruit the most unfriendly people to be at their helm of affairs, the business will definitely be struggling.

Being a walking advertisement for your organization means that at every point in time, you should be marketing your brand overtly and covertly. It is a highly competitive world; do not be afraid to tell people what you do because you never know who might be the next big customer. Carry your business card all of the time with you and hand them out in the most professional yet friendly manner. It has been an enormously successful business strategy for me, time and time again.

Building a golden business for me is firmly anchored in a business that puts into full practice, the tenets of the golden rule in every facet of its life. Well-defined strategic and brand planning are also equally important. It is much more important than the choice of business's name and logo. Strategic planning recognizes where the business currently stands and where it is headed while brand building is a development that creates a relationship between a company, its employees, and its customers. When strategy and branding are done right, the advantages are endless. They bring about profitability, enhance customer retention and loyalty, and enable firms to employ and keep talented employees. All of these in place are great hallmarks of a golden business.

When customers sense a cordial and friendly environment, they would stick out their necks for that business. Customers love a business whose staff members are able to deliver and provide goods and services in an efficient and timely manner. As an attorney managing a small firm, I would always tell my staff that it is my top priority that every client and/or potential client who walks into our office leaves feeling that they truly received top notch customer service.

It is incredible how that translates to repeat customers who often times brings associates and family members after their cases have been closed out. Because of this friendly customer service I advocate in our office, one of our clients ended up linking our firm with up to ten immigration clients in less than a month time frame. I finally came to the realization that the most reliable and effective form of advertisement is word of mouth from a friend, associate or family member. Businesses can spend millions of dollars on internet marketing and if it eventually generates customers that the business is unable to keep, that effort would have meant nothing but a colossal waste of time and resources.

Growing a golden business really does boil down to a firm recognition, appreciation and application of the good old Golden Rule in every facet of a business, especially as it relates to the two core back-bones of every business; customers and employees.

Tamara Jackson is the founder of her own independent literary co. (PBP Productions Inc) and author of Hood Divas, Let Sheedom Ring, Inspirations, The Moment Of Truth, and now co-authoring this magnificent book in the Unstoppable Publishing series with Erika Gilchrist. Tamara expresses her unique talent in her intriguing and inspiring work; she is a native of Chicago, a socialist, and activist in churches and communities throughout the city. She brings her stunning presence by way of positive content through poetry, prose, and other literature. Her motto is, "Helping others helps me," so she is eager to assist all who needs it however she can. Currently Tamara is focusing on establishing a unique foundation for teen girls where she targets and instills self-esteem, self-awareness, self-worth and other positive influence in the youth (girls).

Fulfilling her dreams and aspirations in becoming a motivational speaker, Tamara has explored and taken advantage of many opportunities including writing books, making public appearances and performances. She received major inspiration when she completed an interview with Barbara Schiffman and Camille Leon of Leap of Faith! Tamara has released her sentimental creation, "The Moment Of Truth (A worldwide emergency)" where she pours and shares devotions of prayers, poetry, scriptures and more! She is the founder and creator of the new SOULSPIRATION (a Chicago faith-based development). Visit http://soulspiration-chicago.org for more details.

Contact Information:
Twitter: @ prettybaby81275
Facebook: @ Tamara Jackson
Email: tammyjloves@yahoo.com
Phone: (773) 797-7286
10323 S. Indiana, Chicago IL. 60628

Chapter 19

Believe, Receive, Achieve

Tamara Jackson

One of today's toughest struggles in life is dealing with people who don't believe in you. This seems to be quite the norm for this generation, given that society is fixed on a higher degree of negativity. And despite your growth, you still have the nay-sayers and doubters, as well as those who are supposed to care for you and claim to be supportive of you. The reality is that behind the scenes they may tear you down, and even attempt to sabotage the progress you've already made. But to be a successful entrepreneur, we have to be our own master builders by first believing in *ourselves*.

If you're not careful, the negative things people say will affect you; it will have you down and doubting yourself. Worst of all, it will cause you to give up hope in your dreams and future.

Find your passion in life and if it makes you happy, do not be dismayed or easily influenced by someone trying to change your mind. Listen to your own heart, and just as important, share your dreams with only those whom you trust for genuine support and happiness for you.

Whatever you are compassionate about is confirmation of your dreams, and we should never let anything or anyone destroy them; stay focused and continue to strive, but most importantly believe in yourself!

Mark 11: 24 says: *"Therefore I say unto you, what things soever ye desire, when ye pray, believe that ye receive them, and ye shall have them."*

You have likely heard these statements: "The proof is in the pudding," "Nothing comes to a dreamer but a dream," and "Wake up and smell the coffee!" Although they're quite overused, they do have an underlying quality that cannot be ignored. "The proof is in the pudding" is a way to say that, "To fully test something, you need to experience it for yourself." Before you chose to become an entrepreneur, I'm sure you have been told many things regarding what it was like. Some were likely horror stories, and others tales were beneficial. But as stated above, there's nothing like experiencing it for yourself. "Nothing comes to a dreamer but a dream" means just that, and it's okay to dream, but at some point you want to create and implement a plan that manifests that dream in very real terms. To "wake up and smell the coffee" allows you to see things as they really are so you can draw your own conclusions to select the best choice for yourself.

Believe
What is your dream? What is your focus? What is your heart's desire? What makes you feel successful? Is it a job, a career, a home, or a relationship? Because you are worthy of it, remember God is no respecter of person, and He will grant you what you want, but you must ask, believe, and act on what you are trying to accomplish. Go to that business meeting, communicate with your spouse or lover, and research the pros and cons of a new venture.

There is a route to follow for success - hope, dreams, desire, planning, and execution. And there is a route to failure - doubt, denial, hopelessness, and stagnation - which road will you choose?

Do not be afraid to climb that ladder of success no matter how high it seems, and even if it feels like you have no support, be your own support (by believing in yourself) and surround yourself with those who believe in your vision and want to see you prosper! You were taught that if at first you don't succeed get back up and try again. You see, we sometimes fall but that doesn't mean we have to stay down! In order to be successful and prosperous you will need to have a plan, so draw out a plan, basically a road map to your success!

Start with where you would like to be. Then write down everything that you will need to achieve those things. For example, if you want to open a low-fat yogurt shop, ask yourself what the company's mission is. Then follow through with scouting locations, raising capital, create marketing strategies and hiring staff. Write down as many things as you can think of.

You must be able to carefully balance both business and personal life; maintain the two of them and in doing so, you will increase in both!

What's next you may ask? Well the sequence normally goes as follows: Believe, Receive, and Achieve, and we have covered the believing part, so now it's time for the receiving seed to be planted!

Receive

You may have heard the expression, "It's better to give rather than to receive," and that's true to a certain degree. But let's put that into perspective differently. What if you give *yourself* the time, give *yourself* your best effort, and give *yourself* your all?   You will receive your gift of success!

Picture yourself as a child on Christmas day. Now I know that sounds a bit cliché', but imagine opening that special gift that you've been wanting for a long time. You would no doubt be the happiest kid alive. Well that's exactly how you would feel when you present yourself with that gift of hard work and dedication, which leads to success!

Also remember out of desperation is born progression. When you are desperate to excel and succeed in something, you feel the urge to move and you're eager to accomplish it no matter what anyone says. You have heard that the race is not given to the swift nor the battle to the strong but the one that endures to the end, right?

Well in a race you have a start line and a finish line, now if you start something, in order to fulfill your dream you have to finish it. There is no line in a race that says pause, incomplete, or give up, but endure until the end and finish what you have started. Always remember to stay focused and follow through on your plans. The battle is an uncommon one but if you be strong and fight until the end you will be the successor.

Achieve

What would you do if you had all the resources to make your dreams come to life? What if someone wanted to invest in you? Would you be prepared to move forward, or would it take a day, a week, or a month, or in some cases, a year? We must have that 'ready or not' mentality, that 'go get em' attitude, that 'knock em dead' instinct; so basically if we are ready to reap our success we have to be ready at any given time to give what we've got and if we plan correctly and follow the plans accordingly, we can and will succeed.

Now that you are focused and geared up for that big finale, that blast off, that touchdown, it's time to step into your new you. You have worked so hard in your mind, in your heart, and in your dreams, and most of all you did the work that it took physically to get to that point of no return. Now that you have accomplished so much there is no turning back, right?

We dream of nice big houses, and nice cars, and of being wealthy and all, but seldom do we dream of the foundation; the work that is put into obtaining the nice cars, the wealth, and the big houses. We have to build the foundation to reap the things that we desire in our dreams. When you know that your dreams are for you then you will bring them to pass.

Don't just think it, believe it. Don't just want it, receive it. Don't just dream it do it! Now that you are well on your way to the success you've always wanted, get ready to party, because you are an unstoppable entrepreneur and it is time to celebrate. It's your time to get your blessing so go on and get it.

Can't you just see yourself driving your dream car? Or turning the key in the door of your new home? Or even shopping until you drop and never having to worry if you have money in the bank again? Well all of these things can be yours and more when you believe enough in yourself to start the process.

For example, if you desire to be an event planner, but you're afraid of failing, here's how I would advise you to start:
1. Get a mentor
2. Research other event planning companies
3. Volunteer at other events to study the logistics
4. Determine your marketing strategy

This is how you can RECEIVE your blessings. Map out the things that you desire so you will have something to focus on.

To be a Caterer:
- ➢ Research health codes
- ➢ Decide the geographical parameters of your service
- ➢ How many people do you need on staff?
- ➢ How much will you pay them?
- ➢ Where will you get your start-up capital?

What about that feeling you get from the excitement you get when you have achieved greatness, others are excited because of your accomplishments, when you succeed you inspire others to succeed. I always say helping others helps me, and if I can help in any kind of way (words of encouragement, motivation, inspiration, etc.) I'm on top of it. Allow me to share a story with you: I was suffering from the worst case of depression and insecurity I had ever experienced, but I always wanted to achieve more in life. Knowing that I could be more, and knowing that God had other plans for me, and that I had a greater destiny ahead of me, I then stopped feeling sorry for myself and took a new approach and direction in my life. I began writing poetry to myself at first, and then nationally. And that lead me into writing books, and then I developed a zeal for becoming a speaker, and God only knows what is to come!

I shared that because I wanted to point out that you can start off doing the smallest thing and your blessings will cause that to increase within you. Well we are encouraged to not despise the small things, so no matter how small your task, dream, or resources are you should still dream big and it shall come true!

QueenKay is a mother of two young boys, Chika and Lota, a multi-faceted entrepreneur, writer, enthusiast, and optimist. She moved to the United States from Nigeria when she was 18-years-old. After living in the Washington, DC area for a few years, she relocated to Los Angeles, California. Her desire to realize her creative passions led her to Hollywood. Nevertheless, she soon found herself taking a detour, to follow her heart's pathway. After falling in love and getting married, QueenKay's true-life, fairytale romance ended tragically. Ironically, the ending of her romance was the beginning of her Reconstruction and Transformation and the very catalyst of her First book, *The Reconstruction and Transformation of QueenKay*.

Contact Information:
www.queenkay.com

Chapter 20
Using Technology to Excel
QueenKay

In today's highly competitive world, it is so important to stay in tune with the technology that will help you excel in business. I run a business that was launched in 1998 by my late husband. At the time, I worked in corporate America and supported him in any way I could. Prior to his passing in 2007, he did everything he could to upgrade the systems at the small specialty food retail store so that things like inventory, sales, purchases and transaction reports could be easily assessed. At the time when he was toiling late hours to do this, I thought he was just working too much and wasn't spending quality time with his family.

In retrospect, I am glad he did because I had a foundation to build on when I took over the business. It is important to have some questions answered or start researching the answers as you go along in using technology to excel in your business. Information is important, right? How about the use of knowledge being powerful? How many people really apply the information and knowledge they have towards becoming successful?

Here are some important questions to ponder:

Have you ever thought about starting your own business?
Where do you start?
Are you already in business? How is it going?
Are you passionate about what you are doing?

What are your goals?
What is your productivity and maintenance plan?
What kind of business is it?
Who are your competitors?
What sets you apart from your competitors?
What is your niche?

In November 2007, I became a widow, a single mother of two very young boys and a business owner all in the same day. The African Caribbean Food Market had been in operation for 9 years and had a following of people who were loyal to the business. However, upon the founder's passing, there was a lot of uncertainty that I could run it successfully much less with the passion in which Charles had run it. The business account was in a deficit and there were so many vendors owed. Do I cut my losses, close the business and move to another city and start over? Or do I take this as a challenge; turn things around and see it excel beyond my own imagination? I didn't think too much about it; I stumbled forward and learned a lot of valuable lessons along the way.

So you are a business owner, you want to be successful and you want to use technology to excel, right? Gone are the days when a business could operate without a computer. We are in the age of computers, smart phones, Wi-Fi, the internet, social media, texting, blogging, Facebooking and tweeting. Think about this: "Google" is a verb! No matter how we slice it, you have to stay connected to your clients somehow and engage them because most people have such a short attention span, and if you lose their attention, it's hard to get it back because so many other businesses are competing for it. Where do you start? Whether you are in a service based business, retail, or wholesale you need to have a computer and be part of a network for backing up your data. If you have clients, you need to save their data on a hard drive or server. If you have inventory and you are in retail, you need to have a Point of Sale (POS) set up for accessing very valuable information and also charging your customers.

I will use my business as an example because it is what I know I have measurable success in using technology to excel. Perhaps, you can relate and learn from what I am doing because my business is truly a work in progress and I am fully immersing myself in using technology to excel.

So when I inherited the business, we did not have a web presence. I thought that it would be a good idea to put us on the world wide web. I did a lot of research and found that most businesses with at least a website or page had a higher percentage of exposure and succeeding than those without. In recent years, with the emergence of platforms such as blogging, Facebook, Twitter, and Yelp, it has made it even easier to engage clients and create relationships and interactions with customers. To me, it's important to have these tools available, but it is much more important to know how to use them to really make a positive impact on your business.

Let me define some of these terms to help you understand their importance.

Website: According to Wikipedia, "A **website**, also written as **Web site**,[1] **web site**, or simply **site**,[2] is a set of related web pages containing content such as text, images, video, audio, etc. A website is hosted on at least one web server, accessible via a network such as the Internet or a private local area network through an Internet address known as a Uniform Resource Locator. All publicly accessible websites collectively constitute the World Wide Web."

So with this very important fact, it is important that any business that wants to be easily seen or accessed or to put information out there about its products or services, needs to be on the World Wide Web. Gone are the days when the telephone directory or calling information was enough to get you noticed by your target audience. You really have to make it much easier for potential clients to find your business. In the first few tabs you have to make sure you display who you are, what you do, and how you can be reached. I recently revamped my website for my store by first changing the web address to the store's motto: **www.manmustwak.com** because it is much easier to say and most of our customers identify us by that term. You can still use our store name to find us on the web but it was important for me to simplify things based on the research I did. It is less likely that people will type the web address in error when they are searching for your business on the web when you keep it short. Also, it is important to list your business as much as possible via the major search engines so that your business will appear at the top of the list during a search.

Blog/Blogging: According to Wikipedia, "A **blog** (a portmanteau of the term *web log*)[1] is a discussion or information site published on the World Wide Web consisting of discrete entries ("posts") typically displayed in reverse chronological order so the most recent post appears first."

I started blogging recently on my other website and I have found success with it. I became a published author about a year ago and I had advised by my web guy to blog. He told me that people want to relate to me, and that in order to build credibility and a following, I needed to blog. He said that I would be surprised how many people I would touch and inspire by my write-ups and musings. So I reluctantly started blogging. He set up my wordpress account. Wordpress is one of the many platforms used in blogging. He set it up as a link to my main web site, but to access the site, I would have to sign in directly from wordpress' site. After a few blogs, I realized that this was an interactive way to maintain integrity and relationships with your clientele and give people an opportunity to know what you are truly about. My current blog can be found by clicking on **www.queenkay.com/blog**. For my store front, I am developing a blog that will be incorporated into the website and will have links to my YouTube channel.

That site's address is **www.manmustwak.com/blog**

My store is an African and Caribbean Food Market. We specialize in hard to find food products and spices that folks from those regions are craving and others who have either visited these places or have been exposed to the culture and food are craving. The need became evident when more and more people were requesting recipes for making the dishes and "how to videos" or even cooking classes. The blog will be interactive and informative. People like to know what they are eating, what the nutritional value of the food is, how to make it, and so much more. There will be different foods featured with write-ups and videos showing the preparations of the food. Of course the audience will be engaged and be providing feedback and sharing this information with friends and family. It is important to stay connected with your audience and provide them a value added service that they cannot get from anywhere.

Are you with me so far? Is this making sense? The more you engage your customers, the more loyal they will become, the more referrals you will get, and the more profitable your business will be.

Facebook: According to Wikipedia, "**Facebook** is a social networking service launched in February 2004, owned and operated by Facebook, Inc.[3] As of June 2012, Facebook has over 955 million active users, more than half of them using Facebook on a mobile device."

Think about this, back in the old days, in order for you to be considered part of the "in-crowd," you had to be part of an elite country club costing a whole lot of money and time that you could not afford. But now, if you have the Facebook logo on your business card, a link on your website and a Facebook page, you are looked upon as someone who is in it to win it.

WE'RE ON FACEBOOK!

With this simple Facebook logo, you are letting the world know that you are in business and you are serious about staying connected and relevant. This is an extension of your website where you get to update and interact with your customer base more frequently than you would from your website. Statistics say that almost 1 billion people are connecting on Facebook every day. In fact, a lot of precious time is wasted online as people get caught up in other people's lives as well as getting the dish on the latest fashion and getting caught up on their favorite businesses. If this is the case, why not engage your customers on Facebook as well? That is what I am doing with my store's Facebook page. By simply searching for my business, "Man Must Wak," you get updates on our freshest products, our promos, sales, special new items and so much more. I know for a fact that the customers are engaged because when they call, come to the store, or meet me at a social engagement, they will reference something that they saw on our Facebook page. You are also able to create redeemable offers on your business page so you can measure the success. This is free advertising that you wouldn't get if you went the traditional route. Here you have a captive audience. There is still so much more to learn and utilize by using the Facebook platform to excel in business.

twitter: According to Wikipedia, "**twitter** is an online social networking service and microblogging service that enables its users to send and read text-based messages of up to 140 characters, known as "**tweets**". It was created in March 2006 by Jack Dorsey and launched that July. The service rapidly gained worldwide popularity, with over 500 million active users as of 2012, generating over 340 million tweets daily and handling over 1.6 billion search queries per day. [6][8][9] Since its launch, twitter has become one of the top 10 most visited websites on the Internet, and has been described as "the SMS of the Internet."

Just like Facebook, twitter has a huge following. It is as they call it, "a microblogging social networking service." I recently started a Twitter account for my store and I know that this is just the beginning. Being able to send short messages over this huge platform and connecting with so many customers and potential customers and bringing the traffic to your place of business is incredible. There has never been a more amazing time to be in business. The tools are out there readily available to use. The best thing is that they are free, and even if you have to pay additional for another tier of service, it is minimal compared to what it could be. The most important question you should ask yourself is whether or not you are going to build a strong social networking foundation in addition to your business foundation. You can use twitter to send out brief messages about sales and promos you have going on in real time. You can create a quick buzz that can be measured to see if you are hitting your target market. The possibilities are endless.

It is important for your twitter account to have followers, but it is not the number of followers that is the most important. What is most important is that you have quality-patronizing customers that follow you religiously and believe in your product and your message. Just having the twitter logo on your business card and a link from your website to your twitter page, gives you almost instant credibility in todays fast-paced business world. It is truly an exciting time. However, don't get carried away with all the social media and technology plug-ins and fail to recognize the importance of building a quality brand and a business that has several layers of credibility.

Yelp: According to Wikipedia, "**Yelp, Inc.** is a company that operates yelp.com, a social networking, user review, and local search web site. Yelp.com has more than 71 million monthly unique visitors as of January 2012.[3][4]"

What do people like to do when they go out? Talk about their experience to their friends and family. That is what this company tapped into. I have a yelp page for my business and for the past 2 plus years, I have been contacted by the folks at yelp to enhance my yelp page. They told me that so many people were coming to my store after going on our yelp page. They stated that their analytics showed that clicks to my store's phone number as well as to my store address were going up. At first I thought it was a gimmick to make money off of me and I wasn't having it. I was happy with my free yelp page. After sometime, I did some research and found that the individual user reviews of patrons were just as good as someone referring my store on the streets. That if I could allocate a certain amount of advertising money towards this project while continuing to build my brand and provide excellent customer service, it would be a win-win situation for me. So far, I have been able to track at least 1 out of 10 new customers have come as a result of finding us via yelp.

Again, I reiterate. If you use social media, the way it was designed to be used, then your business would flourish beyond your imagination. The benefits are endless but you have to stay on it. A yelp sticker on your store front or on your website says a lot about your business. You can also interact with the customers and even turn a negative comment into constructive criticism.

In summary here are a few reasons for using technology and social media to excel:

- Generating traffic

- Developing your brand

- Building trust by giving your brand a "face"

- Build relationships with your clients

- Get more leads = more sales

Here are some tips on using technology and social media to excel:

- Always stay on top of what software and hardware programs are important for your business

- Keep your records up to date

- Keep your followers engaged

- Inject your personality, have fun with it – it makes you more human

- Giveaways - do giveaway promos and special prizes

- Ask your followers to share your content

- Utilize the power of videos/video marketing

Technology and social media are always evolving. Some people get frustrated with all the changes, but I encourage you to stay in the know and be focused on your success. Most of the changes are never drastic. Remember, they are in business to stay in business. They want you to be loyal to them so they won't do anything to rock that boat. Do your part and be informed.

See you on the web, "Like" us on Facebook, and I will follow you on twitter!

Darlene Templeton is the CEO and founder of Templeton & Associates. She specializes in transformation and transition specifically for those who want to make a greater impact personally and professionally while rekindling their passion and drive for life. Darlene engages, inspires and empowers women who are overworked and overwhelmed, helping them to put more time back into their lives, so that can do the things that they truly love.

Darlene brings almost 36 years of extensive experience with one of the largest global corporation in the world. She is an executive coach, recognized leader and change agent who brings with her a wealth of experience, including 30 years of management, in the corporate world. She is an "out of the box" thinker and uses her skill to inspire business professionals toward extraordinary results. Fueled by her passion and enthusiasm, Darlene provides clients, teams and organizations alike, the tools for leadership, personal and professional excellence.

She has worked with many organizations and professionals to drive change through leadership and coaching. Darlene is a Certified Professional Co-active Coach (PCC) through The Coaches Training Institute, an Associate Certified Coaching and member of the International Coach Federation (ICF), and a Certified Dream Coach.

Darlene lives in Austin, Texas with her husband, John. She loves spending time with her family and her four grandchildren.

Contact Information:
www.darlenetempleton.com
darlene@darlenetempleton.com

Chapter 21

Breakthrough Leadership Strategies

Darlene Templeton

"Leadership: It's all about YOU!"

What comes to mind when you hear the word *leadership*? With all my years in the corporate world, and having seen *the good, the bad and the ugly* of leadership, my definition is very different from most people.   When I think of leadership, the words authenticity, connectivity, approachable, and "real"   immediately come to mind for me.   This is a person who I want to follow and who I want to get involved with and know more about. They don't have to be the CEO of the company, or the President of the United States, but they do have be someone that exhibits the qualities that are important to me, that I connect with and that they lead with integrity.

Leadership is not about the power of the position. I have worked with and known many people in very powerful positions, and they were NOT true leaders. Dictators may be a better word, but they did not know the real meaning of leadership. You can hold the position, but you are not automatically a leader. This is one of my favorite quotes:

"When leadership is defined not as a position you hold, but a way of being, you discover that you can lead from wherever you are."
~ Roaasmund Stone Zander

If you are like most people, you automatically think of the business or corporate world when you hear the word "leadership." However, the Webster's Dictionary® definition of leadership is, **"The action to lead a group of people or an organization."**

It does not say <u>exclusively</u> business or corporate. You can be a leader in your family, your church, your school, your charitable organization, your business and so many areas in your life. In fact, you are already doing this and may not be aware of it. *Why would you limit this amazing opportunity to just your business?*

Everywhere we look in today's environment, someone is always talking about "leadership," as it's always been the "buzz" word in the corporate world and now in our personal lives. The question that you need to ask yourself is, "What does that mean for me?"

I have asked myself that question many times over the last 36 years, and I always come up with the same answer. My definition of leadership is: "To be successful in all areas of my life, with intention and integrity." So, how do I do that and still be successful in the business and corporate world? I am going to give you some actions and exercises that will provide you the direction so that you can really find out what leadership means to you.

My leadership journey began early in my life as I was always in charge. My first introduction to leadership in the business world was when I was applying for my first "real" job. I was 18, right out of high school and newly married. The job was a secretarial job, which today would be an administrative job, the man I was interviewing with had five children, and his oldest daughter was my age. He said to me, "Your skills and qualifications are excellent, but you don't have any experience." So I stopped, thought about it, and said, "Well, if no one will hire me, how can I ever get any experience?" He laughed, and hired me on the spot. This was one of my first and most valuable lessons in leadership.

I spent almost 36 years in one of the largest global corporations in the world and have seen every type of leaders; *the good, the bad and the ugly.* I managed for 30 of those 36 years, and I truly enjoyed being a manager. I became a student of leadership and I have observed so many outstanding leaders through the years, paying special attention to what makes them so successful. A huge realization was that they were not just focused on the business aspect, but were leaders in every area of their life, and they had attained balance in their lives. I also learned what did not work, and the type of leader that I did NOT want to be. What a valuable lesson!

By applying what I learned from my observations, the role models, along with my own experience, knowledge and wisdom, I am a much better leader now as CEO of my own company and, more importantly, of my life.

Based on my observations and my own experiences, I developed *"Five Strategies to Finding the Leader in YOU."* This is about finding who you are as a leader, and taking the next steps to truly **find the leader in YOU!**

I know, our lives get so busy and too complicated, and you are thinking, "How can I do one more thing in my life today?" I feel exactly the same way, however, when you actually take steps forward to find the leader inside, you will see changes in your life immediately.

- Do you ever feel like your life is leading you?
- Do you feel overwhelmed and overworked?
- Do you want to achieve greater success in your life, both personally and professionally?
- Do you want to make a greater impact on others?

If you answered "yes" to just one of the previous questions, then it's time to take that first step toward your own personal brand of leadership.

There is no set order and the strategies are equally important, so please read through them, and take a moment to see which ones would work for you and fit into your life today.

1.   **Rekindle your passions:** In today's busy environment, "life happens," and so many things that we love to do and mentally plan to do, always seem to take a back seat to the other demands on our time. Between work, family, and our social calendars, there are not enough hours in the day to get it all done. The "mandatory" things always make their way to the top of the list. Take a moment to think about one activity that you are really enthusiastic about:

- Does this activity give you energy?
- Do you love to do this activity?
- Are you truly passionate about it?

Action: **Put that one activity back into your daily routine. Pay close attention to how you feel, and the impact on you, on others in your life.**

2.   **Focus on the 80/20 Rule** – Someone once told me that "Perfect is the enemy of great." We are all goal-driven and want to achieve perfection. These expectations are unrealistic, and actually can have the opposite effect. I just heard last week that, "**Good is the new perfect.**"

- Do you feel that you must be 100% perfect in everything that you do?
- Do you focus on what's not complete or perfect, instead of celebrating what you have accomplished?

- Do you get "stopped in your tracks" when you feel like you have make a mistake?

Action: **Focus on doing your very best 80% of the time, and the other 20% will take care of itself. Realize that no one will know except you, that it is not 100% perfect. Practice letting go of "perfect" and set your goals to be GREAT.**

3.   **Learn from others** - Listening has become a lost art in the crazy times that we live in today. It takes time to really listen and hear what another person is saying. This could be with your family, your customers, your colleagues, your business associates or the strangers on the street.

- Does it seem that you are always the one doing most of the talking?
- Are you thinking of what you will be saying next instead of listening to the other person?
- Do you walk away from a conversation and feel that you really didn't get what they were saying?

To really listen and "hear" what another person is saying, we have to focus on that person, not ourselves.

Action: **Next time you are in a conversation and you are doing all the talking, try this technique and ask yourself, " Why Am I Talking?" or say W.A.I.T to yourself, see what happens, and expect a little magic.**

4.   **Find your balance** – It's even becoming stressful to put balance back into your life, and seems like you need a spreadsheet to keep up with all the things that you are supposed to do to get back in balance.

- Do you sometimes feel that there is no time for you to do anything that you really want to do?
- Do you feel that you are all work and no play?
- Do you just wish that you had five minutes to yourself?

By putting some **"ME time"** on your calendar or somewhere in your day, just for you to do ONLY things that you want to do, you can begin to put some balance back into your life. This can be anything that nurtures you like reading, exercise, meditation, or coffee with a friend.

Action: **Start small with 10 minutes and continue to add more time when you feel ready. Make sure that you keep your appointment with YOURSELF every day, no matter what, like the leader you are. You are important and you deserve it.**

5.   **Choose carefully -** For many years, I didn't know that I had a choice in most areas of my life, especially in the corporate world. I never learned how to say "No," and that became a huge problem for me. "No" is a complete sentence!

- Do you say "yes" when you really want to say no?
- Are you taking on roles and responsibilities that you really don't enjoy or fit with your goals and priorities?
- Do you feel frustrated and angry because you don't have the time to do the things that you really want to do?

You do have a choice, and once I learned that, my entire life shifted. I finally learned that **when you say "yes" to something, you are automatically saying "no" to something else in your life.** Remember that, consciously or unconsciously, you are already making these choices, and therefore you want to weigh those significant decisions carefully, as they might have a lasting impact on your life.

Action: Choose one thing in your life that you will say "no" to and just stick with it. As entrepreneurs, it's very easy to get caught up in doing it all, working 24/7, and living in the "it can't wait" mentality, and we forget about ourselves. Also, for me an overbooked calendar gives the appearance of productive work. That's not true, and that's why putting "no" back into your vocabulary is one of the most important decisions you can make to ensure your success.

I recently took a client's entire team through these 5 strategies and the results were incredible! Each individual team member found the leader within themselves, and the overall team transformation brought outstanding results to the company. Not only did this work increase client satisfaction and employee morale, it also leveraged their strongest asset, their people.

They are now on target to achieve all their goals for this year, plus have found ways to achieve over and above their targets. The most important point is that each person on that team, regardless of their position, job title, or pay grade, has found their passion and their "inner leader," which makes them really UNSTOPPABLE.

These leadership principles also work in your personal life. Recently, we had a very large extended family gathering with eleven children, and four of those were my grandkids. I heard crying and screaming coming from the kids' room, and I went back to see what the uproar was about. What a commotion! All of them were yelling, crying or tattling on the other ones, and the younger ones were screaming. Does this sound familiar? You can change the ages, but could be a scene from a personal or business situation. I was afraid someone was hurt, but what was really wrong was that the video games had stopped working.

I told them all to please get quiet, take a breath, and stop what they were doing. I asked them if anyone had checked this or that, or had tried to fix the game, and no one answered. We had a short discussion on how to first work on the problem before we start screaming and tattling, and then to try to figure out what the next steps are. We all put our heads together and we got the game up and working again and everyone was a happy camper. Surprise, surprise!!!

The next discussion focused on how to be problem solvers and leaders, not complainers and whiners. They loved it, and we were all "high fiving" and "fist bumping" and laughing. For the next two days, all of them were celebrating being problem solvers and leaders. What a change in their attitudes and we did not hear a peep out of them, except laughter and having fun!

My challenge to you is to take a small step and start with just one of these five strategies, try it for a week, and I promise you that you will experience a positive impact in your life and the lives of others. If it worked for my grandkids, then it will work for you.

Once you have implemented one action, and you begin to see and feel the results, choose one more until you have implemented all the five strategies in your life. You will find the true leader within you.

We are all leaders in our lives every day. Acknowledge the areas where you are already a great leader, continue to look for areas where you want to have more leadership, and stay on your own leadership journey.

"Management is about doing the right things; leadership is about doing things right". ~ Peter Drucker

I would love to hear from you after you have started your own leadership journey. This is truly about you and about you finding what leadership means to you.

Leadership: It's all about YOU!

Though increasingly occupied with the many responsibilities of President and CEO, Ms. Clark is still the creative "heart" and driving force of the design boutique started over 20 years ago. With her vision and the many insights gained from the variety of clients in marketing, design and communication, Julie Trotter Clark has formed her business around the core principle of *Marketing Solutions by Design and Branding.*

Ms. Clark began her creative credentials with a Fine Arts Degree from Kansas University, Kansas. She then had the honor of studying with world-renowned Milton Glazer at the SVA School of Visual Arts, New York. Employment with the St. Louis-based Maritz Motivation & Anheuser Busch established her abilities as a creative designer with a solid foundation in business needs and processes.

Among her credentials, Ms. Clark has received many awards for outstanding work & recognition for her clients. She holds a Congressional Award for Entrepreneur of the year, Top 10 2012. In 2006 she launched her own brand into the market with a custom line of jewelry – LesJetons – A Token of Love. She has been a registered WBE Women's Business Enterprise for over 10 years. Her client list says it all, working with some of the best companies in the world. She has been an expert judge in art, graphics, and design competitions throughout the USA. She has taught college-level courses in design and currently lectures on **"Brand" and the creative process at the MBA Level.**

Mother of three and staying involved in both her community and her profession keeps the creative focus a passion not just a job.

Chapter 22

Make Your Business a Brand

Julie Trotter Clark

How to get the WOW into your brand

Why is branding so important? Establishing your brand image is the most important thing you can do for your business. Brand is an element of intellectual property and done properly, it's the most valuable property you can own in today's market. Capturing a market begins with inspiring a single heart and intriguing a single mind. Your goal is to make your company's image stand out to make it memorable. Give it a look and a unique positioning that will provide you with a distinct competitive advantage in the marketplace.

Today, branding is the *one* thing that will set you apart, allowing people to understand who you are and why your product or service is the best. With a unique name, a custom logo, and a distinct positioning statement, you can have a brand image that will be the foundation to your entire business, setting your product and service apart from the rest.

My name is Julie Trotter Clark and I am a design brand expert. For over 25 years, I have worked with some of the biggest companies in the world in establishing their brands. I always remind clients to *"Plan your work and work your plan!"*

In this chapter, I will teach you how to think about your brand, what you need to consider for building a strong brand, and some guidelines and tips you can use.

Where does branding fit in your business?

I typically think of branding as a business in the big picture. All businesses focus on three main areas of concentration. First is *Operations*, the process of making the product or providing the service. Next, there is *Finance*. This is the money and the cash flow, including the prices, the payroll and the profit. Lastly, there is *Marketing and Sales*. Branding fits under the umbrella of Marketing and Sales. If you do not have this part of your company on staff, then you should connect with somebody who can help you. In the beginning stages of your business, it is especially important to get it right and build a proper foundation. Remember*, you never get a second chance to make a first impression.*

The Brand Ladder

In order to climb towards any goal, there are always a series of steps that must be completed before that goal can finally be achieved. The goal here is to create a successful brand that permeates the marketplace and thrills customers. But how do you get there? The "Brand Ladder" is a summary of the branding goals of any company; a series of essential steps that will help the goal become a reality. What are the things you need in your brand toolkit?

The "Brand Ladder" represents the different levels of branding and how effective your brand can be in the market. You can use this ladder in your marketing plan to target growth and measure awareness, with one primary goal ...GET TO THE TOP!

• **The First Step -** *Brand Absence***:**
> Think of this level as the beginning and the initial design development phase. Once your name, icon, identity, and

initial development have been established, you are at the first step. Now you need to tell the world that you are a brand and get customers to take notice. Be diligent about getting it right.

• The Second Step – *Brand Awareness*:

Brand awareness is when customers begin to recognize your name, logo, and tagline. This allows you to initiate a relationship with your customers and inform them of why your brand is better than your competitors. It is critical that you keep the message consistent- be sure to present the same image, tagline and positioning *every time* you have a brand touch point. Far too often, people speak of great advertising but cannot remember the name of the company or the product. Similarly, companies that have complicated explanations of their products or that try to make too many points end up clouding the main purpose of getting a simple message across. Be sure to make *one* single point of distinction. You do not want to be the company that nobody remembers.

Remember to keep it simple and be consistent through all channels and touch points of brand awareness. From answering the phone to taking an order and then thanking someone for their business, always be consistent with your name, logo and message.

• The Third Step – *Brand Preference*:

Brand Preference is achieved when your customers are consistently choosing your product over others on the market because they *prefer* to do so. This leads to **brand loyalty**, when customers think highly enough of your brand to go out of their way to always choose it over others. Once you have established brand loyalty, your customers will be willing to pay more for your product or service because your brand name has become important to them.

•The Fourth Step – *Brand Advocacy*:

Brand advocacy is when your customers start telling other people about your product and recommending it. Your customers will provide the best type of advertising there is- *word of mouth*. When your family or friends tell you, "You should use this brand of kitchen appliance," or, "that type of hair gel is way better than this type," you trust their opinions and the next time you are at the store, you are more likely to purchase that product. This is *loyalty marketing* at work. Studies show that if you have happy customers, they will recommend your brand to an average of three or four friends. However, when a customer has a bad experience and you push them to irritation, this person is likely to tell ten to twelve people not to use your brand. There is nothing more damaging to a company's reputation than bad, complaining customers, whether their complaints are justified or not.

• The Fifth Step- *Brand Insistence*:

You have reached the top of the ladder! Now your customers are your brand leaders- talking, teaching and telling everyone about your brand! The top of the ladder is why customers are willing to pay more for a certain product or service over others every time. Customers tell their friends, share their discoveries and teach what this brand stands for. Think of Starbucks as an example. When you can establish a social change through the coffee people are choosing to drink, you have created a very powerful brand. We see this across many industries with several types of products and services. I am sure each one of us has our favorite brand and no other will do when it comes to dish soap, bath soap, food, hotels, or even airlines.

Putting it all together – *The Brand Toolkit*
What do you need in your brand toolkit?
First of all, you need the marketing plan. Remember:
"Plan your work & work your plan!"

Set your goals
Clear, straightforward communication is the cornerstone of any successful project. Begin with an extensive analysis of your competitive strengths and weaknesses. At this stage, learn everything you can about your target market, your competitors and your risks – set your goals, your unique assets, and begin to plot a forward marketing and engineering strategy for your business.

The Brand Tool Kit is typically in your marketing plan and is a strategic piece of your overall business plan. It includes an overview of your business today and where are you planning to go in a month, a year, 5 years, and beyond. What are the things that will take you there? The list below includes the essential elements for every business brand development; the things your tool kit must have:

Marketing Overview
Scope & Methodology
Brand Strategy
• Name
• Logo
• Identity
Multichannel Marketing Plan
Traditional media - Print
Digital media – Website, Social Media Plan
Measurement Tools

The beginning is a testing period. Large companies spend huge amounts of money in testing prior to getting a new product into the market. However, over the last several years, the onset of the internet has changed everything and even just a small business operation with only several people can blossom overnight and become a serious brand. Make sure that you are ready for this and that the blossom is not a bust. Be ready for spontaneous growth or you can lose your business before it even gets started.

The first items in the tool kit are the name, logo and positioning statement. This will also consist of the color, the typography, the look and feel - it is the essence of what the company needs to communicate about the product or service.

Depending on whether your company offers a product or a service, the items will differ in the list of what is needed. A product business will need packaging and labels, whereas a service business will need a brochure explaining the process or the kind of service offered.

The identity package consists of a business card, electronic letterhead, notecard, brochure, folder or press kit, label, the initial web home page, and the template for the type of digital presence that best suits your business goals. The template of your digital presence will include items such as mobile applications, email marketing, social media campaigns, and blogging. You should also consider using direct mail, publication ads, billboards, and YouTube commercials.

I like to consider a business card as a billboard. Be sure that it stands out and is memorable. People will appreciate a unique look and they will surely follow up the next time they need your product or service if your business card speaks to them.

Naming

Your brand can ultimately be the most valuable thing your business owns. There are five different types of naming categories and trademarks that you can protect. The first and most distinctive names to protect are **FANCIFUL NAMES**; they are the easiest to protect because they are made-up words. They do not exist until you create them. What is a Kodak or an Exxon or a Xerox? These are all words made to be brand names. We all know and identify with these names because the companies they represent have spent significant time and money establishing their identities and their brand essences.

The next naming category consists of **ARBITRARY NAMES.** These are words that exist but have nothing to do with the product or service offered under the name. The brand has given the word a different meaning from its dictionary definition. Examples include brands like Apple and Macintosh for computers and Lotus for software. We all know that an apple is a fruit and that a Macintosh is a type of apple, but advertising has established a new meaning for the word, as we also know that Apple is also a brand of computers.

The next category includes **SUGGESTIVE NAMES**. These names suggest something about a quality or characteristic of the product or service. There is a link between the brand and what is offered for sale under it. What we are to understand for the brand essence is communicated by the brand properties. Examples of suggestive names are common, such as Microsoft (software for microcomputers), Edge (shave gel), or Tilex (bathroom cleaner). The name suggests the product's attributes, functions, or purpose.

The fourth category of naming is classified as **DESCRIPTIVE NAMES**. These names describe the way the product performs and behaves. They are the least protectable and weakest names for products or services. This is because they describe a quality or characteristic of a product or service. An example of this type of naming is including the word Lite if the product is a light beer. While it may seem like a good idea to choose a descriptive name, you may not be setting yourself apart from your competitors and your potential customers may not be able to find you.

The final naming category commonly used by businesses is called **GENERIC NAMING**. You *cannot* protect these types of names with a trademark because they are the names of the product or service. A generic name is what we describe the item or product as when we communicate about what it is. These names include words like umbrella, slippers, or flowers.

The laws for trademark are established for the purpose of consumers' clarity and protection from confusion when they are purchasing something in the marketplace. It is important to check the legal status of the name you choose and to get it properly registered when you begin. I recommend consulting a trademark lawyer who can evaluate whether your proposed brand name is available for your product or service.

It would be a huge mistake to start a product or service line and not get the proper paperwork in order to operate your business. This could result in losing your name and hard work because somebody else did the legal homework and can send you a cease and desist letter, demanding that you close your business or change your name. This would be a very costly mistake.

Once you think of a great name, conduct research to determine whether or not it is available. After you learn that it is available as a trademark, be prepared to spend the money that it takes to immediately pay for your name online. It only takes a quick web search to figure out if the *.com* of your brand name is available. When you figure out that it is available, be prepared to buy the website immediately. This is very easy and a fundamental first step.

If you do not purchase it right away, it may not be there the next time you search. Web crawlers see the search and buy it, and the next time you search for it, it could cost hundreds of dollars. Remember that you will want a name that describes the purpose of your business and is easy to remember, because that is how people will find you on search engines.

So how and where do we start?

Consider two things - the written message and the visual message. In these messages lies your brand with your unique positioning statement.. This is often referred to as the USP or the POS. This is the supporting copy that describes *exactly* how you want to communicate the difference of your product or service from your competitors.

The WRITTEN message is the NAME and the USP.
The VISUAL message is the ICON or the LOGO.

Logo Design

I think of the actual name and logo as the logic of the brand, or what Aristotle would refer to as *logos*. This is the logic, the *why* of your brand. It is the logic that will become reality in the marketplace. It's a written message with a visual, and will establish your brand's essence. Remember to *make it different*. This is your unique identity that should communicate clearly how your product or service is better than anybody else's.

How Your Brand Needs to Communicate

For this section I will refer to the **Gestalt Theory**. Gestalt is a psychology term, which means "unified whole". It refers to theories of visual perception developed by German psychologists in the 1920s. These theories attempt to describe how people tend to organize visual elements into groups or unified wholes when certain principles are applied. These principles are:

Similarity
Anomaly
Continuation
Closure
Proximity
Figure and Ground

Similarity occurs when objects look similar to one another. People often perceive them as a group or pattern. When similarity occurs, an object can be emphasized if it is *dissimilar* to the others. This is called **Anomaly**. When one in a series is different, it stands out and is visually distinctive.

Continuation occurs when the eye is compelled to move through one object and continue to another object. Continuation is often used in web design, because the viewer's eye will naturally follow a line or curve. The smooth flowing crossbar of a design leads the eye directly through what is being communicated.

Closure occurs when an object is incomplete or a space is not completely enclosed. If enough of the shape is indicated, people perceive the whole by filling in the missing information. The design is not complete, but enough is present for the eye to complete the shape. When the viewer's perception completes a shape, closure occurs.

Proximity occurs when elements are placed close together. They tend to be perceived as a group. When nine squares are placed without proximity, they are perceived as separate shapes. When the squares are given close proximity, however, unity occurs. Though they are still individual shapes, they are now perceived by the viewer as one group.

Figure and Ground is when the eye differentiates an object form its surrounding area.

A form, silhouette, or shape is naturally perceived as *figure* (the object), while the surrounding area is perceived as *ground* (background). Balancing figure and ground can make the perceived image clearer. Using unusual figure/ground relationships can add interest and subtlety to an image.

Anybody can design a logo, but to make it right, *you need a professional!*

The Logical Left

So, how do we make that connection? How do we make our brand stand out and really *matter* to customers? Well, the big secret is how our brain works and how we can affect who we are talking to in our brain function. There's a logical left brain and an emotional right brain. Our brand answers the question of the logical left but the connection is actually in the emotional right. So we want to make an emotional connection with our brand - we want people to be attached to us through what their passion is and why we want to be connected.

PUTTING IT ALL TOGETHER

Remember, a strong brand makes an emotional connection. You want to communicate the brand's distinct advantage, so tell your story in unique and creative ways. Using unusual typography and color causes people to associate what your brand means with simple, clear, consistent communication. Tell your story. Have fun when it comes to creating the strategy of your brand. Remember to *plan your work and work your plan.* Do not be afraid to test, test and test some more. The business environment today is like never before. One day you can be nobody and in a very short amount of time your business can be off the charts. Be prepared! Have an implementation and action plan in place. Build out your brand with both traditional and digital media. Be creative and consistent!

Watch for more information on design and how you can make your brand better!

Or contact me for more information or how to get your brand on the road to success. I would be happy to see how I can help.

www.JTClark.com
Julie@JTClark.com

An inspiration speaker and entertainer, Patricia has been accused of "doing it all." As a concert pianist she has performed in Branson, Grand Ole Opry, Atlantic City NJ, and Southern California. She has pedaled 9,000 miles since age 67, raising $36,000 for kids to further her passion for scholarships. Reigning as MS.Sr.CA '06 and Ms.Sr.NE'08, she finished in the top five in Las Vegas and Atlantic City, where Mayor Evans proclaimed her "The Official Bicycling Beauty Queen". She was selected as Nebraska's Ambassador for sports and fitness award in 2010. She served as cover girl and a four-page featured article in Radius, a Health Magazine's September 2011 issue. 37-27-37 measurements at age 75. She taps; drives a big red moving van; has a "hole in one" on a Jack Nicklaus designed course; a nutritionist; a "cougar"(20-year younger husband); high fashion, ramp and photographic model; an actress; a director and teacher; singer; pipe organist; trombonist; a professional tiler; landscape designer; a Delta Zeta and a Red Hatter.

Meet Patricia the author, <u>Angel on My Handlebars</u> chronicling the agonies and ecstasies of pedaling America in short shorts and Hanes pantyhose as an angel put its wings around her for an hour while she pedaled through a horrific thunderstorm by the Grand Tetons. A six page adapted chapter in an ESL textbook published by Thomson/Heinle and CNN is used worldwide. She won a coveted 1st Place Award in Memoir from the prestigious Santa Barbara Writer's Conference; has extensive TV coverage including FOX live in St. Louis, Denver and Washington DC, newspaper and magazine print. Lastly, she's inviting you to enjoy the next chapter about how to get your "warm fuzzies" Read on! www.patriciastarr.net

1-402-443-1774 964 N. Laurel, Wahoo, NE 68066

Chapter 23

The Joy of Entrepreneurship

Patricia Starr

The big "E" doesn't always have to revolve around money or your own business prowess. Did you ever think about how you will be remembered when you leave this earth? It won't be for the Lamborghini you were driving, or the figures in your bank account. When your mind is churning down the path to financial freedom and recognition from your peers, it's easy to think that once you have completed these goals, you will live happily ever after.

But, wait a minute! What if all the accolades of success don't bring you the "warm fuzzies" that make memorable moments in your life? How do you implement your actions to experience the enjoyment of the complete circle of success?

True happiness is achieved when you experience the euphoria of giving back to someone else. This is the underlying tenet of the 12-step program that has succeeded internationally for over 75 years.

My goal is to jump start your imagination. Now your ingenuity steps up to the plate. The following are suggestions for bringing joy and meaning to your business along with ways to build a solid reputation in your community:

1.   Use your business expertise

Do you own a software business? Contact the Boys and Girls Club. Everyone needs computer knowledge, and the kids can polish their leadership skills by teaching you a shortcut or two. In turn, you can encourage them to use their new-found information to make money in the business world.

Do you own a beauty salon? Have your customers enter a drawing. Pick half a dozen teens to receive complimentary hair and cosmetic makeovers for prom night. Set up a drawing at a retirement home and offer your services to the lucky winner. Do it weekly or monthly as your schedule allows. Many retirees don't have the extra cash for personal luxuries.

Do you own a skating rink? Offer free classes and organize competitions to encourage kids to improve their skating proficiency, physical fitness and self-esteem.

Do you own a graphic design and/or printing business? If so, you are probably a whiz with publicity. It can often be a struggle to get crowds to an event, no matter how good the program is. Since someone has to get those seats filled to reward the musicians and actors for their hard work and to pay expenses, your expertise in providing marketing materials can have a major impact on the success of the event.

2. Share your own individual talents

Are you a musician or performer? Offer to perform at the retirement homes in your neighborhood.

Check out the local churches. There are many outstanding music programs and the directors love to have leaders in their choir sections. These are occasionally paid positions. Either way, you get the enjoyment of being with dedicated people that have a specific goal: spending time to make something beautiful happen.

If you live in a city fortunate enough to have an orchestra, most have music vans that go around to the local schools and familiarize the kids with the various instruments. If you have played an instrument in high school or college, you can help demonstrate. If not, but are willing to help, they always need volunteers to assist with set up and even drive the van. Opportunities are endless if you start thinking where and how you can donate your services to help someone else.

If you are a music lover but not a performer, volunteer to usher at the symphony or other musical programs in your area. You not only get the reward of helping, you also get to enjoy the entertainment for free. What a deal!

Are you a speaker? Contact the local Lion's Club or other service agencies as they are always looking for guest speakers.

Are you a reader? Check into the Braille Institute. Recording for the Blind wants you! Devote several hours a week reading aloud in a recording sound studio. Imagine how the world opens up to someone who can then experience what we take for granted--being able to pick up a book and read for enjoyment or instruction. I've done it. It's easy and fun.

Are you an athlete? The after-school programs for kids include sports. Volunteer to teach your favorite sport or help coaches on the basketball, golf, soccer, track, or swim teams. You will impact many lives; make contacts; cultivate new relationships; and enjoy more exercise, all while giving back to your community.

Check with local colleges and offer to do an inspirational talk for some of their classes. Forget the $10,000 fee you might be paid and enjoy the kids.

Are you an author? Contact the local high schools and ask to be a guest speaker in their English Lit and/or Composition classes. The kids have probably never met a "real" author and maybe the teacher hasn't either. Can you feel the excitement in the classroom?

Are you a tutor? You can be and may not be aware of your value. Any of the Boys and Girls clubs and after-school programs have children that can benefit from your assistance. They get behind in school and cannot catch up on their own. Sometimes, families don't have time to help. Enter the tutor. You can turn a student's life into something productive instead of one on the streets. They need the basics, but most importantly, they need a one-on-one relationship with someone who cares and will spend time helping them. A couple of hours a week can change some child's life forever. Think about it!

3. Utilize your hobbies or interests to enrich someone else's life

Are you a good cook or maybe even own your own restaurant? Find a live-alone neighbor or shut-in and bring them a gourmet meal once a month (with plenty of leftovers!)

Check with a local nursing home and ask the supervisor if there is a resident without a family (probably more than one) and make a date to visit once a week. Good conversation and caring fellowship are easy to give and you can be the light of someone's life! Bring a friend so two people can receive this marvelous gift of love.

Call the local Cancer Society and offer to do an inspirational talk. They lean on each other for support but welcome visitors who are leading lives unaffected by illness. You bring them hope. They loved it when I read excerpts from "Angel on My Handlebars," my book about pedaling across America. It momentarily took them along with me to experience some of the crazy, and sometimes scary, adventures that continually happened on the road.

Do you have a pet? Hospitals and retirement homes want you if you have four-legged friendly ones, but maybe leave your boas and iguanas at home. Can you imagine the joy of being able to touch a furry friend that has come to visit YOU! Such a simple gesture we all take for granted, but when one is institutionalized, that privilege isn't available anymore. They love someone else's pet for the moment and enjoy the connection to an animal that will love them back unconditionally. One of my California neighbors had three golden retrievers that were visitation dogs. Two of them actually retired from their careers after many years of bringing happiness via a wagging tail. Their beautiful golden coats with their silver noses enabled them to fit in perfectly with the age of many of the recipients. The younger one is still bringing cheer to the grateful patients.

Have you ever had a secret desire to be a clown? Now's your chance! What fun designing the most outlandish costume you can imagine. You will be welcomed with open arms at any hospital or care center, kids after-school programs, retirement homes or parades. The ideas and possibilities are endless! The satisfaction you receive bringing joy to others of all ages is priceless.

Join a group--a church, Lions Club, Toastmasters, Assistance League. It will not only improve your social life but every organization needs volunteers to make their wheels turn. Your contribution is invaluable.

How about giving your time and assistance at the local soup kitchen that feeds the needs of the less fortunate? There, but for the grace of God, could be you or me. Holidays are especially difficult for the homeless. You can help by donating a few hours.

On occasion, our actions or information can be the solution to someone else's needs. Contact colleges and universities where professors often need to publish new material and are constantly looking for ideas. When I was pedaling across America, we got a call from a teacher at Santa Barbara City College who was publishing a book but needed a final chapter. She was a substitute in our tennis foursome and knew about the ride. She interviewed me by phone and included a six-page chapter in her ESL book adapting the information in her workbook pages. Her problem was solved and my ride was published by Thomson/Heinle and CNN and used worldwide.

Consider being a "pink lady" at your local hospital. No, you do not need to empty bedpans. Your duties include front desk service assisting visitors with directions, working in the gift shop, being a hostess in the cafeteria, delivering and watering flowers, and all the extras that need attention. My friend, a teacher, retired after being a pink lady for 30 years because she needed to care for an ailing husband. Imagine how many lives she touched over all those years!

If you have children in elementary school, being a room parent gives you an A+ in your child's eyes. Be observant. Some children are sad when their parents can't or don't attend the functions. You can love yours, but spread that special attention to some other child, too.

Volunteer for the Special Olympics events in your city. Many supporters are needed to help the physically and mentally handicapped add some enjoyment to their challenging lives. This is a service of pure love.

You may be wondering where I get my "warm fuzzies." Because I have been a professional musician all my life, I've shared my music teaching and playing skills gratis, as well as being a paid performer and instructor.

When the seeds started to grow and mature concerning my ride across America and we knew it would be a reality, the next thought was: *If I was going to tackle something spectacular at retirement age, someone should benefit from it.* Gabriel was an alcoholic (now sober for six years), so attention focused on a local organization in

Santa Barbara that has helped many kids survive their teens and twenties with drug and substance addictions. The organization's reputation was spotless, and the creator and funder of the program was an icon in the community. It should have been a perfect fit for our dreams to raise money for something that was successfully making a difference for many kids.

We set up an appointment, took the promotional goodies with us that we had started working on, and sat down to talk. As the meeting progressed, we learned they followed their own strict guidelines. We sat there with beautiful colored brochures in our hands but they only used a one page black and white copy with no pictures for publicity purposes. We had photographers who would do videos and other promotional materials at a reasonable price, but they only used their person, who charged many thousands of dollars.

Many other items were discussed, and all was cordial as we got up to leave. After we walked out the door, I turned to Gabriel and said, "My stomach hurts. That doesn't feel like the right fit for what we want to be doing, spending our own money and giving up three months of our lives." Gabriel agreed, "I felt exactly the same way, and their approach gave me knots too." End of story!

That night I sat up in bed at 2 a.m. and wondered, "What about my life?" I was able to get an education because someone cared. Their thoughtful deed enabled me to have a fabulous life as a teacher and performer. My flying fingers have played piano in Branson, Grand Ole Opry, Atlantic City, New Jersey, Las Vegas, Laughlin, Palm Springs, Southern California, Canada and many places in between. Fox 'Live' in Washington, DC featured me on a morning show last summer to share information about my 4,000-mile ride around America and I had the opportunity to play Chopin on national television. What a thrill!

Our quest was over. Nothing could be a more passionate gift than establishing scholarships so I could give back. My first 3,622-mile bicycle ride across America at age 67 raised $22,000 and funded a $1,000-a-year perpetual scholarship at Santa Barbara City College. The second 1,400-mile ride was from Wahoo, Nebraska to Atlantic City, New Jersey to compete in the Ms. Senior America Pageant, which raised $14,000 for the kids at Wahoo High School.

The 4,000-mile adventure at age 74 was to encourage people to set up scholarships in their own communities for their kids and the beat goes on. Beware! You may get hooked on the "warm fuzzies" like I did. There's the Tour de Nebraska bicycle ride in my future. I'm only one person but I am making a difference. So can you! Gabriel and I are opening a much-needed Kids Fun Center in our town of Wahoo, NE. How simple it is to give!

The miracle of giving is that you also receive. On the ride across America, my world came crashing down upon the discovery that our van was stolen from a Holiday Inn parking lot at 6 a.m. My dream for the kids started to crumble as I had already pedaled over 3,000 miles and could not let that happen. With tears streaming down my cheeks so fast I could hardly see the pavement, I got back on that bicycle. The thought of those kids missing out on scholarships held me together as my physical and mental worlds collapsed around me.

This is only one chapter, but I could write a book! Now it's up to you. The choices are endless. Do some exploring to find your perfect, passionate fit. Keep looking around and listen to your heart (and stomach). Sometimes it takes some investigation to find your niche; however, you may find several!

Remember also the tiny warm fuzzies that should be totally entwined into our lives. My husband and I opened "Love it Again," an Antique Mall in Wahoo. A woman visited the mall, fell in love with a desk and as she lived quite a distance away, called to say she wished to purchase that beautiful piece of furniture. Our manager and I talked to her several times to settle details and arranged the out-of-town delivery. She kept insisting on speaking to Gabriel who was out of town for the day. Could it be that she only wanted to deal with the "head man" to discuss her purchase? When Gabriel returned her call that evening, she expressed her desire to speak to him personally because they had been at an auction together. Gabriel had heard her mention a painting she really wanted. As the auction progressed, that particular item was grouped with the things Gabriel had the highest bid on. When the items were brought to him, he pulled out the painting, turned to the woman, handed it to her and said, "I heard you speaking about this and how much you wanted it and I wish to give it to you." She offered to pay him but he would not accept anything.

Her "urgent" calls to Gabriel were to again thank him for his kind deed and to reiterate how much it meant to her. Can we possibly know all the lives we touch by our thoughtful actions, large and small?

Let the ripples continue into eternity...

Ethel Maharg is the former mayor of the Village of Cuba, New Mexico, where she served in office for 10 years, three terms as mayor. She was the first elected woman mayor of Cuba. She has been privileged to address many audiences, such as the Sandoval County tourism conference, and has shared the same platform as Governors Gary Johnson, Bill Richardson, Senator Tom Udall, and in Washington Senators Pete Domenici and Jeff Bingaman.

Ethel's greatest passion is to help you discover yours. She loves to speak to audiences that desire to improve their station in life. She provides inspirational leadership training to help people in the achievement of their personal and professional goals.

Her mission is to empower individuals to find their purpose, and equip them to pursue it. To make a difference in every life she touches. She challenges everyone to live a life that is uncommon.

Ethel is an alumnus of University of Phoenix where she received her degree in business administration. She has owned and operated several small businesses, been an educator, worked with unions, and managed two branches for Wells Fargo.

Ethel is a proud member of the National Speakers Association, the Hispano Chamber of Commerce, and currently serves on a Women's Leadership Team for Women's Leadership Development at New Beginnings Church of God where she is an active member. She is a keynote speaker as well as a trainer. Her audiences love her openness and her no nonsense humorous approach. Ethel resides in Albuquerque, New Mexico with her husband of almost 28 years.

Contact information:
mayormaharg@hotmail.com

Chapter 24

Being a Shameless Self Promoter

Ethel Maharg

As the old saying goes, "If not me, who; if not now, when?" These are two questions you want to ask yourself as a shameless self-promoter. Let's start with the first part: "If not me, who?" - No one has more at stake than you when it comes to ensuring the success of your business. If you don't promote it, no one else will—I promise you. The next question is, "If not now, then when?" A friend once told me you don't have forever to get something done. Life is short, and if you blink, it's over and the opportunity is gone.

Being a shameless self-promoter is an intriguing topic because almost immediately it conjures up visions of arrogance and cockiness. Having served in public office for ten years, I wanted to make certain that I was not a glory hound, but in the private sector, being a shrinking violet may be problematic or even deadly to a business because, as stated earlier, if you don't promote yourself, who will? Often, I do what I do without having to promote myself. On the morning I was scheduled to be interviewed on the radio, I simply did the interview. Do you think I told anyone? Uh, no! Later, friends told me that they had heard the tail end of the show and wished I had let them know I was going to be on. I had become so accustomed to doing my work without seeking recognition, that it had become a habit, and for my line of work, that kind of habit isn't always a good one.

It's OK to self-promote. Let me repeat that. It's OK to self-promote. Not only is it OK, but it is imperative. If you don't tell the world about your great product or service, who will? You understand better than anyone what you are passionate about. People are too busy with their own lives to seek you out, so you have to become the proverbial squeaky wheel that causes them to remember you at the time they need what you have. You have to be like a jingle in their heads, like McDonald's, "You deserve a break today."

Profit is not a dirty word; there is no shame in pursuing it. The first responsibility of any company is to make a profit. Why? It's simple: If you do not make a profit, you are out of business. Without a profit, you cannot pay employees, keep the lights on, pay suppliers, and so on. Therefore, becoming profitable is job one. Being "rich" has been frowned upon by some, and unfortunately, our government has vilified it by wanting to tax those who have achieved certain levels of financial success. I do believe that everyone is responsible for paying their fair share, but individuals who have worked diligently to grow a business should be rewarded—not punished—for their accomplishment. The success of Steve Jobs is one example of a company that was extremely profitable. Through his creative genius and tireless efforts, his contribution to our society has changed the way we all do business today.

To provide the best information about being a shameless self-promoter (SSP), I sought out three of the most accomplished people I know and asked them what it was that made them successful. I conducted three interviews with identical questions.

The first phenomenal guest is Augusta Meyers, and according to PEAK LIFE HABITS®, Augusta Meyers is a powerful keynote and workshop presenter. She is a communications specialist and delivers our very special "keynote workshops" to delighted audiences. She is an Emmy award-winning journalist and television anchor who has spent sixteen years at KOAT-TV—the ABC television affiliate.

The next person is Jim Hakeem. Jim has more than twenty years of experience in the Albuquerque real estate market. He has a Bachelor of Science degree in mechanical engineering from New Mexico State University and management certification from the University of Notre Dame. For the twenty years prior to entering the commercial real estate profession, Jim owned a successful food manufacturing company that he sold to open his own real estate investment partnership.

The final guest is the Rev. Dr. Richard Mansfield. Dr. Mansfield is the senior pastor of New Beginnings Church of God in Albuquerque, New Mexico. He studied business at the University of Texas in El Paso, and in 2011, he was named Albuquerque Police Department Chaplain of the Year. Prior to that honor, he received the 2008 New Mexico Governor's "Rev. Richard A. Mansfield" Proclamation and the 2008 National Day of Prayer City Coordinator Twenty-five Year Service Pin. If anyone knows about being an SSP, these people do, so it is my privilege to share what they had to say:

Q1: What do you think it means to be a shameless self-promoter?
Augusta: "We have these God-given talents in us that we can act on and that we are good at that God gives us and that we bring to the table of life. A lot of times you hear those negative voices that tell you that you can't do it that you aren't pretty enough, smart enough, you don't speak well . . . whatever; and you've really got to hide those voices in your head. I think about being an SSP-you have to know that what you have to say or promote is really worth it. Once you decide that, and you believe in it and you believe in yourself, you will be able to talk about it- to present it -and the decision you made. Then—and only then—can you go forward with it. You're committed to doing that. Once you decide that OK, this is what I

believe in, this is what I do, you've got to do it. You've got to put it into action."

Jim: "Making sure that you identify people's needs. It's so important to understand them and put them first and yourself second. You just have to do that, and in this industry, it has been the other way around. When you begin to think about you first and your clients second, you can be compromised and that is what you don't want to happen. Sometimes it may be at a sacrifice. At the same time you are promoting yourself it comes across how you are treating other people, and if they are being treated on a priority basis, you've self-promoted."

Richard: "An SSP is someone who has really discovered what their passion in life is and what makes their heart beat. They have discovered what their gifts and talents are. They have discovered what and why they wake up in the morning, what they wake up to do and why they wake up to go do it. They have discovered what they really love about life and they're doing it. They have had a real self-discovery. For Richard it all begins with bringing people to Christ, because now you know your creator, now you can know why you were created. Once you find out who your creator is, you find out why you were created. You find purpose, direction, and meaning. You find passion and drive, You find what you want to do, how you want to do it, why you want to do it, and with whom you're going to do it."

Q2: Do you consider yourself to be a shameless self-promoter? Why or why not?
This question caused them to pause a bit because, like most people, they had never considered the question and, for most, it comes with a negative connotation.

Augusta: "I could be better at it. I do have a shy side. Sometimes I have to really push myself to put it out there. I fall victim to the same thing that everyone else does . . . that inner voice that says you can't, you're not good enough, you're too old, not smart enough, not pretty enough— but for the most part, I'm good. I just have to fight it. When I decide I really want to do something, I'm like a bird dog. I either stay on it until I get it done or I figure that I can't do it. That is what helps me overcome my own fears, my own insecurities. Once I decide then . . . I think it's like that for everyone in life. It comes down to how bad do you want it? You want to lose that last ten pounds; you want to run a marathon in your life. How bad do you want it? You will get your butt out of bed to do what you need to do if you want something bad enough."

Jim: (After a long pause) "Yes, because I am good at what I do. Most importantly, I feel confident about what I do, and I feel good about myself. I can walk in to or out of any establishment, any office, and I know that I have not burned bridges that I would ever be concerned. Obviously, you're not going to make everybody happy, but I am very confident, very knowledgeable about my industry, and I feel good about myself. When I put my jacket on every day and walk out, I'm ready. I am ready."

Richard: "I had never, ever, ever, ever thought of that before you asked. I am reminded of successful people, and they all are quick to point out the fact that they stand on the shoulders of those who they took with them, -people brought them to this place. Wow, I never thought about it. I try to live my life transparently and point them to who I am because of Christ. I am not ashamed of the core values that I live by, and they always pull me back. Therefore I promote these values. Those things that you espouse will keep you accountable."

Q3: What makes you a shameless self-promoter?
Augusta said, "One of the keys to my success in that area is my relationships with people."
Jim pointed to his forty-one years of relationships with people.

Richard said that people often tell him he is very passionate, to which he says, "I am; now, let me tell you why." (It opens a door to self-promotion.)

Q4: Do you think it is important to be a shameless self-promoter? Why or why not?

Augusta: "It's important to be a SSP because that's your message and you're the vehicle that takes it out to the rest of the world. Really craft your message. Get good at it, and people will not only understand what you're saying, but they will care about it."

Jim: "Absolutely. It is one of the building blocks to success. It is the opportunity to keep moving forward."

Richard: "We should always be very proud of who we are."

Q5: Do you think it is arrogance or confidence that allows you to be a shameless self-promoter, and why is that important?

Augusta: "Confidence is much better than arrogance. Just face it: People like to be on a winning team, and when they see a confident person, they want a dose of what that person has."

Jim: "When you are arrogant, you don't care. When you are confident, you know what you have to do to promote yourself with dignity and character."

Richard: "We all have a certain self-reliance, and for me, it is God-reliance. Self-reliance is relying on self, but you know who self is. People get arrogant when they feel that they don't learn from others. They are no longer humble and think they don't need other people."

Q6: Can you be humble and a shameless self-promoter?

Augusta: "Sure. It's important to be humble. It sometimes is refreshing to an audience to have someone not know all the answers, when they stop for a moment to think about it."

Jim: "Humbleness is an important trait; it creates comfort. It breaks down barriers that are created or are perceived. It brings down walls."

Richard: "Being humble is the greatest achievement. It is the expression that we need God and the expression that we need others. I didn't get there by myself."

Q7: Do you think that men are better self-promoters than women? Why or why not?

Augusta: "Men are often projected as the leaders; women are more subtle, and more powerful in their subtly. It really isn't whether they are men or women; it is about when they are really good at something."

Jim: "Not better. In some industries the number of women compared to men is lopsided. Women have more responsibilities."

Richard: "No. Women are better SSPs, but they aren't aware of it. Men size each other up by what do you do for a living. 'Do I outrank him, or does he outrank me?' A woman immediately begins to ask things like are you married and do you have any children? Men are better self-competitors. Because of it, they are SSPS/competitors. Women are better at building relationships."

Q8: How do you think that it benefits your clients if you are a shameless self-promoter? What value does that add to them?

Augusta: "I'm more likely to get hired, or rehired. If I do a good job for them- if I help that company or that person be successful. It is important that you are a SSP for your clients; that's how you are getting paid."

Jim: "You add value to your clients."

Richard: "Knowing that I am dealing with an expert at what they do makes you glad that you are doing business with them. Showing the confidence you have in your ability gives the client security knowing that you are the best. It takes you to a whole different level of doing business with them. When you are dealing with the best, it gives you confidence to do business with them, knowing they know what they are talking about. It gives you faith and you feel like you can place your trust in that person."

Q9: What would your advice be to someone who wants to be a shameless self-promoter but doesn't quite know how to get started?

Augusta: "Get some books—for example Richard Branson or Les Brown. Listen to some motivational speakers. Everyone is reached by different people. The other thing is to listen to history. Study the history of people that lived hundreds of years before us that had mountains to climb and obstacles to overcome. One person in particular that influenced me was Christopher Columbus. He could converse with the lowliest of people on his ship and then with the Queen. He spoke the language of so many people. He humbled himself, he learned them."

Jim: "Establish trust, relationship experience, and industry knowledge. Know your industry and people will cling to you. Humbleness. Find out what works for you."

Richard: "Have a solid identity of who you are and know what you want to do. What is it you want to promote about yourself? What is it that you're good at, and if you're good at it, have you honed your abilities and talents and taken them to a better level? Are you the best you can be? Are you teachable, are you moldable? There has to be the finding of self and the finding of purpose and then doing everything you can to hone it, to perfect it so that when you are doing it, you know you are right where you're supposed to be."

I could have filled the pages of an entire book with the wisdom and knowledge of these fine people, but I only get one chapter, so . . .

I would like to summarize what was said as well as what I have learned over the years of promoting myself.

1. **Find your purpose**. You can go around in circles if you don't determine what you were meant to do. And yes, you are meant to do something special. Often, the best way to do that is to ask yourself what you are you good at, what you love to do, and what you would continue to do even if you didn't get paid.

2. **If you have discovered what you are destined to do, do everything necessary to improve your craft.** If you want success in your business, you will want to become the best in your field. If you are promoting a product, know everything there is to know about it and how it will benefit your clients. Knowing your industry gives you confidence, and when you have confidence in yourself, others will also have confidence in you. As Augusta said, you will cause them to care about your message.

3. **Promote relationships more than your product or service.** Remember: People do business with those they like and respect. B. J. Thomas wrote a song that says, "Using things and loving people brings you happiness I've found, cause loving things and using people only leads to misery." Truer words have never been spoken. Gone are the days of the salesperson who twists your arm to make a sale. If you want more business, build more and better relationships and learn to speak the language of everyone, just as Columbus did.

4. **Remain humble**. No one likes to be around someone who has a bad case of larger-than-life ego. Remember: You didn't get where you are by yourself. Make certain that you thank those who helped you along the way.

Finally, when you have discovered what it is you are meant to do or be, you have taken the time to perfect your craft, and you are well-liked and humble, give it the gas! Go ahead and tell the world about what you have to offer, and do it with abandon. After all, if you don't, who will?

www.ingramcontent.com/pod-product-compliance
Lightning Source LLC
Chambersburg PA
CBHW060329200326
41519CB00011BA/1885